Johnson's®

feeding your baby

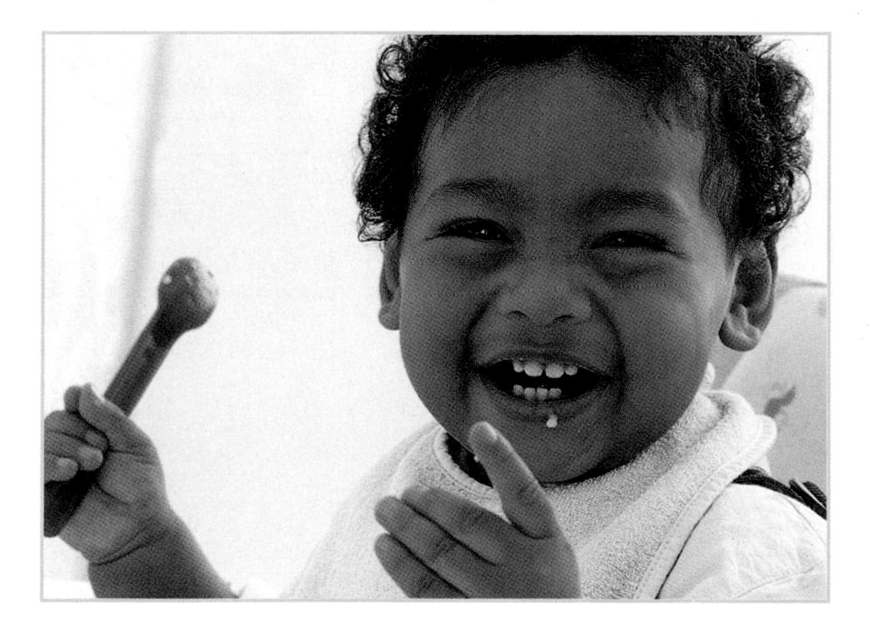

London, New York, Munich, Melbourne, Delhi

Text by Tracey Godridge
For Cora, Eden and Noah

Senior editor Julia North
Senior art editors Glenda Fisher, Hannah Moore
Project editor Angela Baynham
Project art editor Alison Tumer
DTP designer Karen Constanti
Production controller Heather Hughes
Managing editor Anna Davidson
Managing art editor Emma Forge
Photography art direction Sally Smallwood
Photography Ruth Jenkinson

Category publisher Corinne Roberts

First published in Great Britain in 2004 by
Dorling Kindersley, A Penguin Company
80 Strand, London, WC2R 0RL

Reprinted 2005

2 4 6 8 10 9 7 5 3

Every effort has been made to ensure that the information contained in this book is complete and accurate. However, neither the publisher nor the authors are engaged in rendering professional advice or services to the individual reader. The ideas, procedures, and suggestions contained in this book are not intended as a substitute for consulting with your healthcare provider. All matters regarding the health of you and your baby require medical supervision. Neither the authors nor the publisher shall be liable or responsible for any loss or damage allegedly arising from any information or suggestion in this book.

A CIP catalogue record for this book is available from the British Library

ISBN 0 7513 3887 7

Reproduced by Colourscan, Singapore
Printed by Star Standard, Singapore

See our complete catalogue at
www.dk.com

A message to parents from Johnson's®

The most precious gift in the world is a new baby. To your little one, you are the centre of the universe. And by following your most basic instincts to touch, hold and talk to your baby, you provide the best start to a happy, healthy life.

Our baby products encourage parents to care for and nurture their children through the importance of touch, developing a deep, loving bond that transcends all others.

Parenting is not an exact science, nor is it a one-size-fits-all formula. For more than a hundred years, Johnson & Johnson has supported the healthcare needs of parents and healthcare professionals, and we understand that all parents feel more confident in their role when they have information they can trust.

That is why we offer this book as our commitment to you to provide scientifically sound, professionally reviewed guidance on the important topics of pregnancy, babycare and child development.

As you read through this book, the most important thing to remember is this: you know your baby better than anyone else. By watching, listening and having confidence in your natural ability, you will know how to use the information you have in your hands, for the benefit of the baby in your arms.

PETIT BATEAU

Contents

"I love breastfeeding Eve. I'm also **excited** about giving her some solid food. She already enjoys **sitting with us** at mealtimes."

LIZ is mum to five-month-old Eve

1

Getting ready for solids

Breast milk is the perfect food for your baby for the first year. But, as she grows, milk alone is no longer enough. For healthy physical development your baby needs to learn how to eat solid food. This is also the first step towards feeding herself and joining in family meals.

Why does your baby need solid food?

As your baby gets bigger she needs more calories to maintain her rate of growth. If she stays on a diet of milk alone she'll have to feed more often and her needs will not be satisfied.

Solid food can give your baby the extra calories she needs without filling her up too quickly. It can also give her the extra nutrients her body now requires. For example, from six months your baby's natural supply of iron is starting to dwindle. Iron is vital for healthy growth and milk alone cannot provide her with enough.

Introducing your baby to solids is also her first step towards enjoying healthy food and discovering that sharing meals is fun. Your baby is becoming more independent – she is learning how to sit up unaided and to grab what she wants; she loves to put things in her mouth, and she wants to be included in everything. Learning how to eat solid food and joining in family meals is the next step on her journey to independence.

When to start

The recommended ideal age to start getting your baby used to solids has traditionally been between four and six months. However, experts now believe that babies need nothing more than breast milk for the first six months of their lives. If your baby seems dissatisfied after her usual milk feed and is less than six months old, try to satisfy her by breastfeeding more often or talk to your health visitor. Whether you are breastfeeding or bottle-feeding formula, around six months weaning should commence.

In order for your baby to accept, swallow and digest solid food certain physical developments need to occur:

- loss of the tongue-thrust reflex – at birth your baby naturally pushes anything that goes into her mouth out again with her tongue, but between four and six months this reflex disappears
- development of her jaw and tongue so she can move food to the back of her mouth ready to swallow
- development of coordination and head control so she can maintain the posture needed for swallowing
- maturity of the gastro-intestinal tract so she can digest different foods
- the ability to cope with a larger volume of food in her tummy.

Checklist

Your baby needs to start eating solid food because:

- milk alone can no longer satisfy her physical needs
- her stores of iron are running out so she needs an additional source
- eating solid food is fun – and your baby wants to be one of the family!

Is my baby ready for solids?

Your baby will be ready for solids some time around six months of age. There is no hard and fast rule – as with other skills, such as sitting up or crawling, some babies are ready to move on earlier than others. The deciding factor should be your own baby's needs and development. If you are unsure, talk to your health visitor or GP.

Don't start too soon

Until the age of six months, all your baby's nutritional needs are met by your breast milk. Between the ages of four and six months your baby loses her natural tongue-thrust reflex (see page 7), and as her digestive system matures she will become able to cope with solid food – waiting until six months is especially important if you have a family history of allergies. Once she is approaching this age, start to watch out for the following signs.

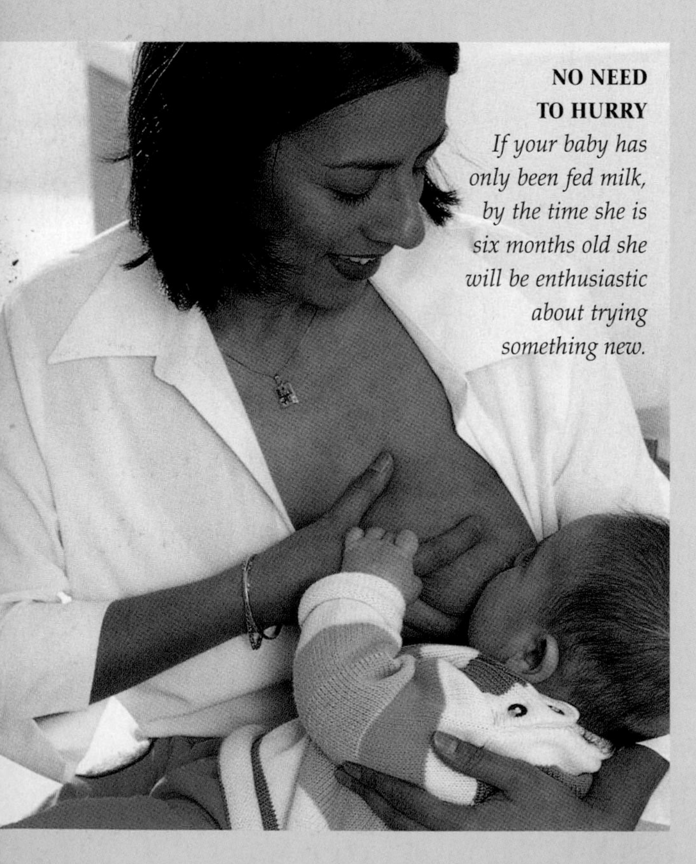

NO NEED TO HURRY *If your baby has only been fed milk, by the time she is six months old she will be enthusiastic about trying something new.*

★ She seems more hungry than usual

When your baby starts shortening the length of time between feeds or even starts waking in the night for an extra feed, chances are she could be ready to give solids a try.

★ She can hold her head up well

Your baby needs good head control before she can safely be given puréed foods, otherwise there is a risk of choking. By now she should be able to lift her head properly when she is propped up or strapped into a reclining chair.

★ She's interested in the food you eat

Watch your baby at the table. Is she following each bite you take? Does she look as if she's imitating you chewing? Does she make noises and wave her hands as if saying "Hey, can I have some?" By six months most babies are expressing a desire for solid food.

What about premature babies?

If your baby was born early, you need to be careful when calculating her age for starting solids. Avoid introducing them until at least four to six months after her due date rather than after her birthday.

"THAT LOOKS GOOD!"
When your baby starts showing interest in your food, you can be sure that she's getting ready to try some solids herself.

Delaying the introduction of solids much beyond six months may cause problems later on as teaching older infants to chew can be difficult. In addition, your baby may not be getting all the nutrients she needs from milk alone after this time. Consult your doctor or health visitor about when to start if you are unsure.

Once you feel your baby is ready to start solids it's important to go at her pace. Your baby will – like all other babies – discover how to lift her head, swallow purée and eventually hold her own spoon and feed herself. But she is also unique and will do these things only when she is ready.

Your baby still needs milk

Your baby is not ready to give up the breast or bottle just because she starts eating solid food. To begin with she'll simply be getting used to new tastes and textures and much of what you put in her mouth will come straight back out, so she

*"Ben, my eldest, was a **hungry baby**. Within a couple of weeks of starting solids he was devouring everything in sight. Thomas was more laid back and took longer to get going – but now he loves mealtimes as much as his brother does."*

JAN is mum to Ben, 5, and Thomas, 3

still needs her full supply of breast milk or formula. In fact, this will be an important source of nutrition for her until she is one year old.

Experiencing solids

For your baby, tasting solids for the first time is an incredible experience. When you offer her her first tastes you are doing a lot more than just giving her the nourishment she needs – you are stimulating her senses in a way she has never experienced before.

- **Taste**

From an early age "tasting" is a way of exploring and as soon as your baby is able, everything within reach will be mouthed – although she may not always like the taste! She was born with a full set of 10,000 taste buds and, while they take some years to mature fully, she can already tell the difference between sweet and sour.

- **Smell**

Just as babies prefer sweet tastes, they also prefer sweet smells such

HEAD CONTROL

Your baby's ability to hold his head up without support is a key sign that you will be able to start feeding him solid food before long.

as vanilla and banana. In fact, your baby's sense of smell is so acute she is able to tell the difference between your breast milk and that of another mother. Smelling is another way in which your baby learns about the world around her – and giving her new foods offers her the chance to discover new smells.

- Touch

Feeling things with her mouth is one of the most important ways your baby has of exploring and learning about her environment. And food teaches her a lot about texture – it can be soft (mashed banana) or hard (a cube of cheese), rough (a rice biscuit) or smooth (a grape). Even a runny purée feels strangely different to your baby's mouth compared with milk.

READY FOR MORE
During her first few months your baby will change dramatically, not least in making the leap from a milk-only diet to eating solids.

Questions & Answers

Members of my family suffer from asthma and eczema. Does this affect when I give my baby solids?
Your baby is more likely to be prone to allergies if they already exist in the family so it's best to be cautious (see pages 54–55). Waiting until your baby is at least six months old before introducing solids can help prevent allergies occurring.

How are allergies caused?
While your baby is young, her gut is more porous, so proteins (the parts of food that cause allergies) can leak into the bloodstream. Your baby's immune system reacts to these proteins in the way it would react to germs. Then, whenever she eats that particular food, her immune system reacts as if it is an infection. She has what is called an "allergic reaction".

Why does it help to wait until six months before introducing solids?
The older your baby is when she first tastes real food the more mature her digestive system has become. The proteins are less likely to leak into the bloodstream and your baby can handle different foods without having an allergic reaction. Also, her immune system is more mature and better at recognizing the difference between a food protein and bacteria. Exclusively breastfeeding until your baby is six months old may not prevent her developing an allergy, but it can reduce the likelihood and severity. In babies who have no solids before six months, allergies appear later, tend to be milder and the children grow out of them earlier.

"I'll **never forget** the first time I gave James baby rice – my husband took a **memorable photo** of him smiling at me as he had his first taste of solid food."

RUTH is mum to James, six months

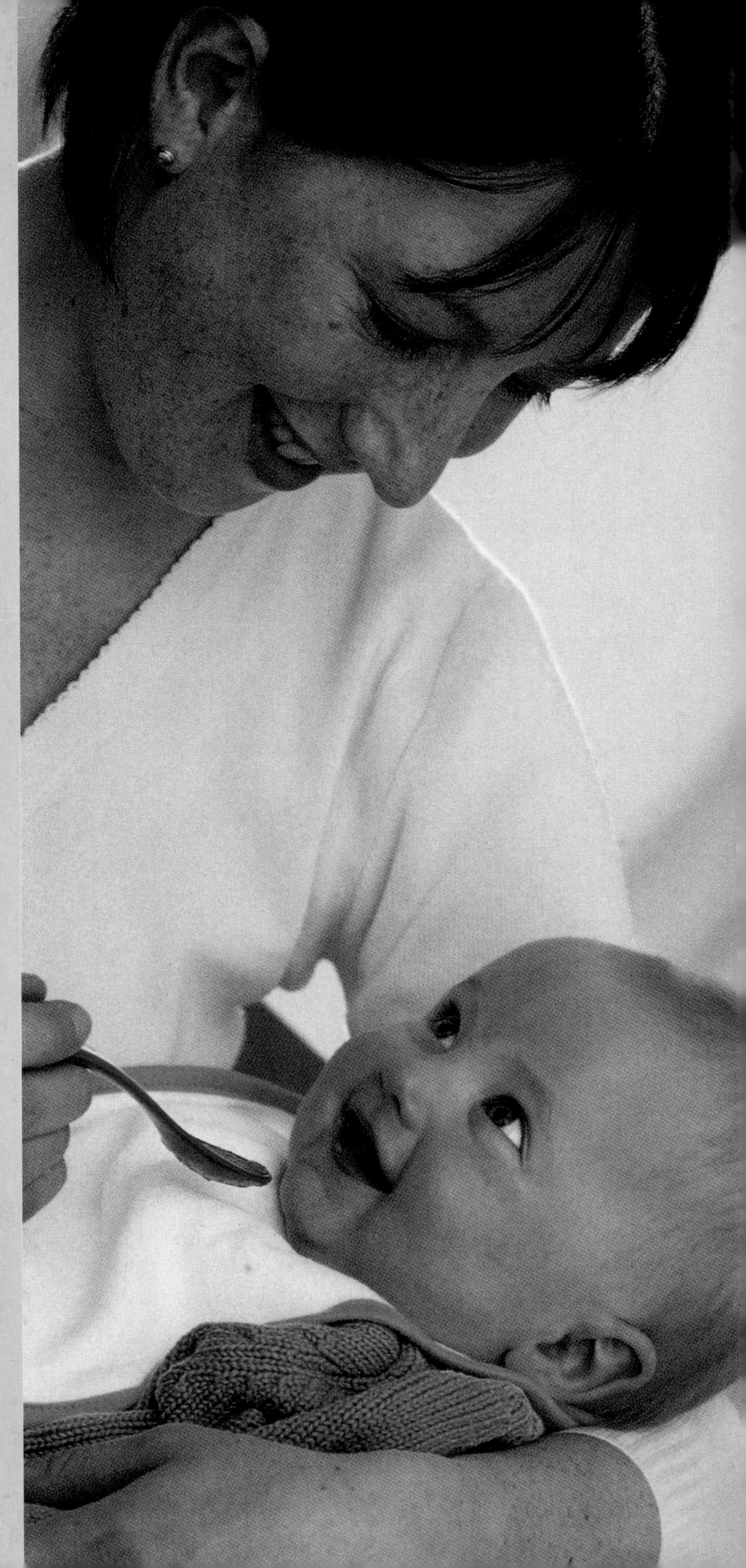

First tastes

Giving your baby his first taste of solid food is an exciting moment. But his first tastes are more about experiencing something new rather than gaining extra nourishment. Being prepared – knowing which foods to serve, and what to expect – will help the moment go smoothly. Here we look at what you will need and how you can make your baby's first experience of solid food a happy one.

Be prepared

Your baby's first taste of food is a major milestone in his development and one you need to be ready for. Once you decide that the time is approaching when you will introduce solids, it's worth preparing for the big moment so you can feel calm and in control as you offer your baby his first mouthfuls.

You'll need to make a trip to the supermarket to buy your first few items of baby food. But don't go overboard. Remember, at this stage you are just offering your baby his first tastes of solid food and it may be a while yet before he's on three meals a day.

What you will need

For preparing food you will need:

- a nylon chopping board (wooden boards can harbour germs)
- one of the following for puréeing food, depending on budget: a nylon or steel sieve and a plastic and nylon or stainless steel spoon; a mouli (hand-turned food mill); or a small hand-held electric blender or food processor
- a steamer – good for fast cooking to preserve nutrients
- plastic containers with airtight lids for storing food in the fridge
- ice-cube trays for freezing surplus food in convenient small portions
- freezer bags for storing frozen cubes of purée.

For serving food you will need:

- lots of soft fabric bibs (easy to wear and easy to wash) and a plastic bib with curved bottom designed for catching food (especially useful once your baby starts feeding himself)
- a set of plastic bowls – unbreakable and easy to wash
- plastic teaspoons with soft or rounded edges – easier on your baby's tender gums.

Where should my baby sit?

You can sit your baby on your lap or strap him into his baby seat or car seat, preferably placed on the floor for safety. If he still can't sit up unaided, he will need to be slightly reclined – but he should be upright enough to eat and swallow without choking.

Great expectations

Lots of parents have a camera ready to record the moment when their baby has his first taste of solid food – but don't expect too much! Remember that this is the first time your baby has tasted anything other than milk.

Which are the best first foods for my baby?

Until now your baby has experienced food only from the breast or bottle, so to begin with the best foods are those which are most like breast milk or formula. He'll be happiest if the food you offer has a bland milky taste and a runny consistency so he can easily suck from the spoon. His digestive system is still immature, so first foods should be gentle on his tummy, too.

Baby rice

Most babies start with specially made baby rice. It has many benefits:

★ it only needs mixing with breast milk or formula or a little cooled, boiled water

★ it can be easily thinned to a texture not much thicker than milk

★ it can be easily digested

★ it is unlikely to trigger an allergic reaction as it is gluten-free (see pages 28–29)

baby rice

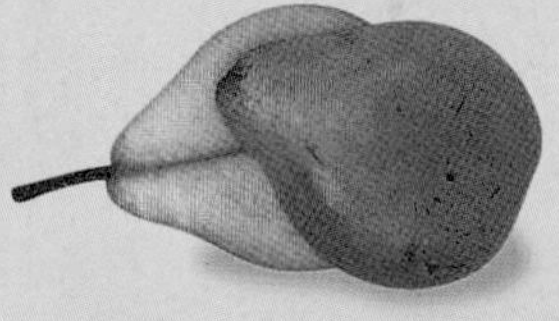

pear

carrot

Baby rice is enriched with iron, reserves of which may be running short.

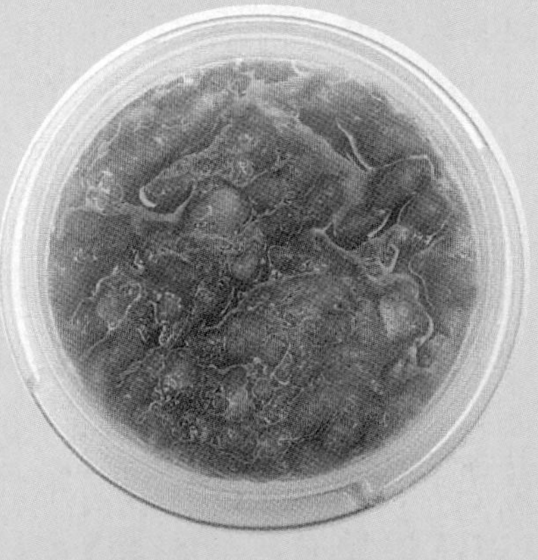

Pears can be stewed then puréed and are rich in vitamin C.

Puréed carrot is popular as it has a sweeter taste than green vegetables.

★ it is enriched with iron which can be easily absorbed (exclusively breastfed babies in particular might be needing an extra boost of this - see page 7)
★ it tastes reasonably familiar with the addition of breast milk or formula.

Fruit and vegetable purées

Fruit and vegetable purées may taste more unusual than cereals but lots of babies seem to prefer them to baby rice. They are also unlikely to cause an allergic reaction. It's a good idea to try vegetable purées before fruit purées because your baby will naturally like sweeter tastes best, so if you start with fruit you may find he tends to refuse less sweet foods.

Try carrot, potato, sweet potato, parsnip, swede, stewed pear or apple, banana, melon and mango. Avoid giving all yellow or orange vegetables because this can cause some babies to take on an orange/yellow colour.

Getting the texture right

First solid foods are not really solid at all - in fact, they need to be semi-liquid and as much like milk in consistency as possible so they are easy to swallow. You can make up baby rice with cooled, boiled water, but breast milk or formula will give it a familiar taste and make it more acceptable to your baby. Purées of fruit and vegetables will also need to be thinned down using cooled, boiled water, breast milk or formula.

Banana is simple to prepare as it can be mashed; it is also easy to digest.

Puréed potato is a popular first food as babies like its bland taste.

Sweet potato, like carrot, is often more palatable to babies than green vegetables.

The new taste and texture will probably baffle him and, chances are, what goes in – if anything does – will roll straight back out again!

As with all skills, learning to eat food takes time and practice. Your baby will go at his own pace, but there is much that you can do to encourage his interest in food.

- Let him sit on your lap at family meals so he can see everyone enjoying their food.
- As he becomes more adept at using his hands he'll love playing with food. Let him squish a piece of cooked pasta or dip his hands in some yogurt.
- Talk to him while you are preparing his food – whether you are getting ready to breastfeed, fixing a bottle or getting his solids ready.

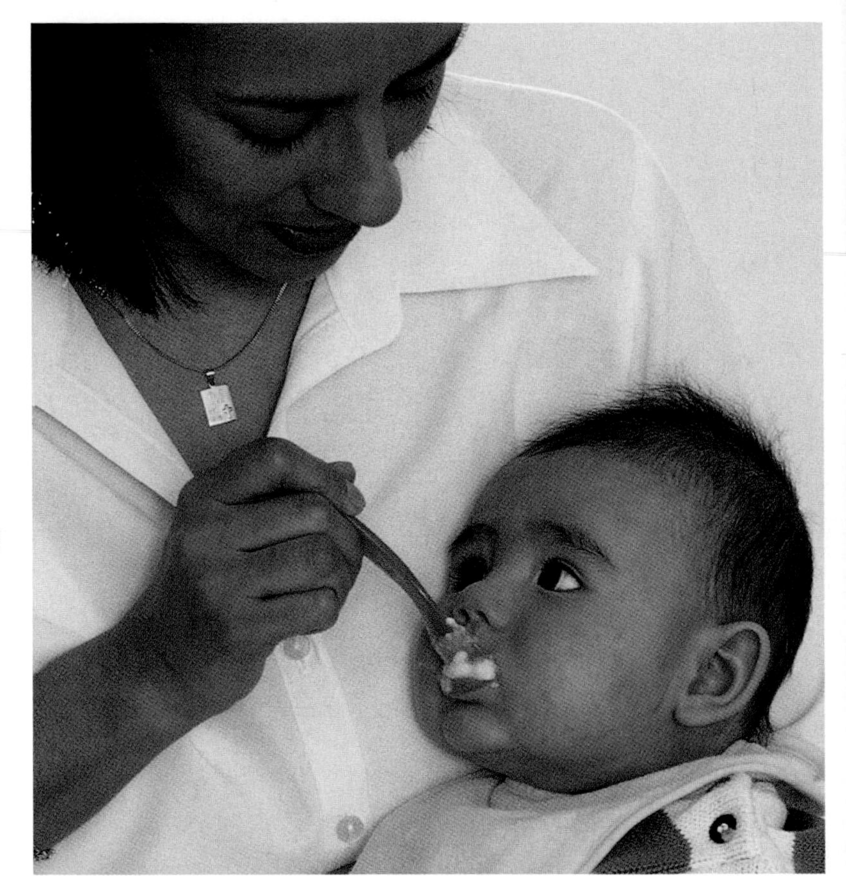

How to give the first feed

- Talking to your baby all the time, prepare a small amount of food using the methods described on page 20. Then give him up to half of his usual milk feed to take the edge off his appetite.
- Sit him on your lap or in a baby seat or car seat. Using a plastic spoon, place a tiny amount of food in between his lips. Don't push it in too far or your baby may gag. And don't worry if he pushes it straight back out – he'll soon learn how to suck food from the spoon. A tiny amount will stay put and you can scoop the remainder up and slip it back in.
- Give your baby lots of loving attention – chat, smile, tell him how wonderful he is. Make a point of touching him and stroking him whenever you can to help him feel safe and secure.
- Try another spoonful but don't expect him to take more than a couple of tiny teaspoons. Don't worry if most of it ends up smeared around his face – he's discovering what it feels like and is more likely to let you try again if he is having fun.
- Once your baby has had enough he'll turn his head away, close his mouth or lean back.
- Tell him how clever he is and give him lots of cuddles. Finish up with the remainder of his milk feed if he's interested.

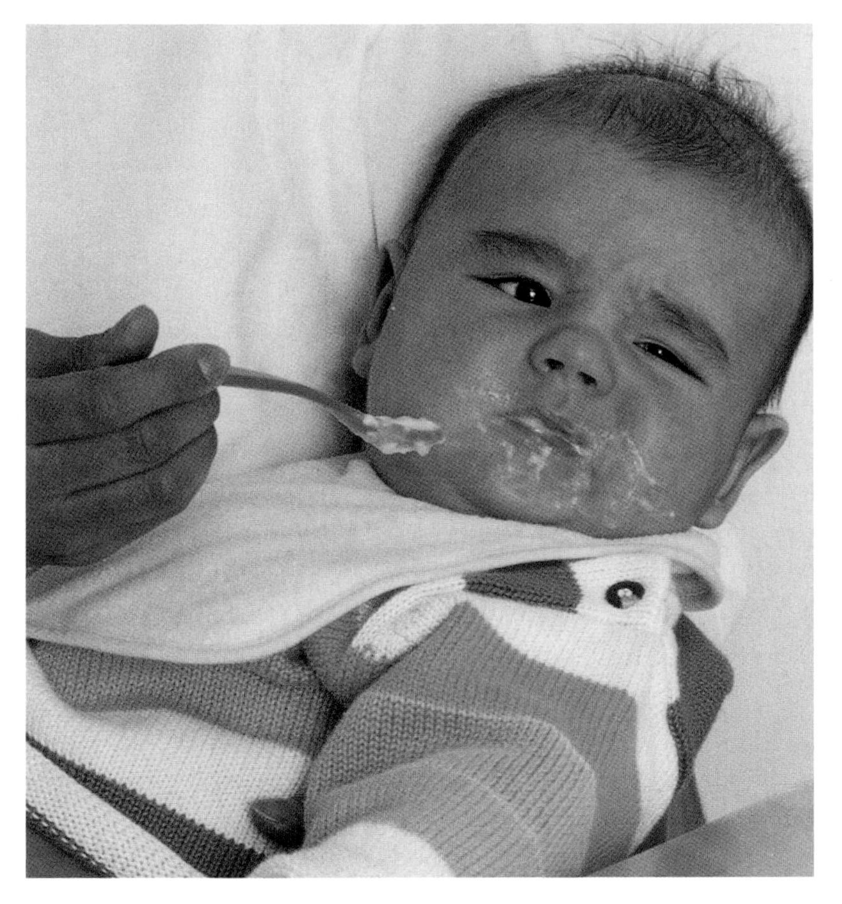

Expert tip

It's not unusual for a baby to gag if he is offered a food he doesn't recognize, too large a mouthful or a texture that's slightly thicker than normal. Gagging is a protective reflex – it helps get the food back to the front of the mouth where it can be spat out or repositioned. Try thinning first foods a little more if your baby gags. All food, however, can cause choking so it's vital never to leave your baby alone while he has food or drink in his mouth. Talk to your health visitor if gagging or choking become a regular occurrence.

A WHOLE NEW EXPERIENCE
Give your baby tiny amounts of food at a time to begin with. When he has had enough he will close his mouth and turn his head away.

Tell him what you are doing and praise him for watching. He'll love your attention and learn to associate mealtimes with happy occasions.

A new skill to learn

Once you've decided that today is the day for giving your baby a taste of something new, get everything ready beforehand and choose a time when you are both feeling happy and relaxed. Introducing new foods takes time so it may be worth putting on the answering machine and forgetting about other chores while you give your baby your full attention.

Most babies screw up their faces with surprise no matter how much they like the new tastes. So how do you know whether your baby loves or loathes the food you are giving him?

- If he likes it he'll open his mouth for more, in which case you can continue to offer him a few teaspoons each day, gradually increasing the thickness of the purées.
- If he doesn't like it he'll turn his head away, cry or won't seem interested. Don't worry – chances are today is just not the day. Try again tomorrow. If your baby still isn't keen, wait a few days before giving it another go. If he still isn't keen talk to your health visitor.

Don't be worried if your baby is finding it hard to get the hang of eating solid food – until now he has always taken his food by sucking, and learning how to feed from a spoon needs lots of practice. His tongue-thrust reflex (see page 7) is only just starting to disappear and

Trying new tastes

Some babies are naturally reluctant to try new tastes. Here are some ideas to help you both.

- Serve your baby's food at room temperature or slightly warmed.
- If your baby rejects the spoon, dip a clean finger into the food and let him suck the food off it.
- Try offering some food after a shorter breast- or bottle-feed than usual. If he's alert but not over-hungry he may be keener.
- Don't make up too much – ready-to-mix baby cereal rather than ready-mixed gives you the option of using tiny quantities.

often the food you give your baby will simply dribble out because he doesn't know how to get it far enough back on his tongue to swallow.

Give him only a tiny bit of food, holding the spoon close to his lips. If he likes what he tastes he'll soon discover that by sucking he can draw the food off the spoon. Sucking will also help him get the food to the back of his mouth so he can swallow it.

When your baby has had enough, he'll close his mouth or turn his head away. However much is left in his bowl, don't force him to take any more – your baby needs to decide for himself whether he's still hungry and which foods he likes. And while, at this stage, it's hard to tell whether he's rejecting a new taste because he doesn't like it or is still mastering the art of eating, it's better to be cautious than pushy.

What to avoid

Never add any of the following to your baby's food:

- salt – this can overload his kidneys
- sugar – this can encourage a sweet tooth
- honey in liquid or solid form – it can contain spores that cause infant botulism: the digestive systems of babies under one year old are immature, and spores can germinate and cause disease.

DAD'S TURN
Starting on solids provides a great opportunity for dad to get involved with feeding.

PASTA PLAY
Allowing your baby to handle solid food will help him explore and get used to different shapes and textures.

Don't be tempted to mix baby rice into your baby's bottle. Adding cereal to bottles risks over-feeding your baby and can cause choking. Also, it's important that your baby gets used to the mechanics of eating: taking a spoonful, resting, taking another and stopping when he's full. Experiencing first foods in this way will help your child develop good eating habits which will last him a lifetime.

Nappy changes

Once you start introducing solids you will notice the consistency and colour of your baby's stools changes. They will be more solid, darker and probably smellier! This may come as a bit of a shock - especially if up until now your baby has been totally breastfed and his nappies fairly inoffensive. The change is perfectly normal. His digestive system is still immature and the food often doesn't change much in between going in and coming out again.

If your baby's stools become hard, you notice him straining, or there is a reduction in the number of his stools each day, talk to your health visitor as your baby may be constipated.

Questions & Answers

When's the best time of day to give my baby his first foods?
Your baby needs to be relaxed, not too hungry and not too tired. Early morning and late evening may not be the best times as your baby might be hungry, half awake or half asleep. He may be more cooperative mid-morning and late afternoon. Watch him closely and feed him when he's happy, hasn't had a milk feed for a while, yet isn't too hungry.

Will starting my baby on solid food help him to sleep through the night?
Lots of parents imagine that introducing their babies to solids will help them sleep through the night. Research shows that this isn't the case. Babies routinely wake in the night – even when they are not hungry – and until they learn how to comfort themselves and fall back to sleep on their own, they are unable to sleep for extended periods of time.

My baby just isn't interested in solids. What should I do?
It's much more important at this stage that both of you enjoy mealtimes, and if, despite your best efforts, your baby isn't keen to give solids a go, don't force the issue. Instead, go back to breast- or bottle-feeding exclusively for a few days and then try again. If you have concerns, talk to your health visitor.

How should I prepare my baby's food?

Preparing simple purées made from fruit and vegetables for your baby needn't take long – and it's less expensive than shop-bought baby food. With a few simple precautions and cooking tips you can give your baby safe and healthy meals. You can also easily prepare small quantities in advance so they are ready to hand when your baby needs to be fed.

Making your own purées

Try to cook fresh fruit and vegetables within a day or so of buying them.

1 Wash and prepare the fruit or vegetable and cut into even-sized pieces.

2 Steam or boil (use as little water as possible to preserve the nutrients).

3 When soft, allow the food to cool a little then purée using a mouli (hand mill), food processor or hand-held blender. Alternatively you can push it through a sieve.

4 Test the temperature of the food on your fingertip or arm before giving it to your baby – room temperature or slightly warm is best. Babies' palates are very sensitive, so be careful not to burn your baby's mouth.

HEALTHY COOKING
Using a steamer to cook your baby's food will help preserve the nutrients which are normally lost during the cooking process.

PUREEING YOUR BABY'S FOOD
A hand-operated food mill is ideal for puréeing your baby's cooked food. This stage won't last for long so don't buy an electric blender or liquidizer specifically for this purpose.

PREPARE IN ADVANCE
You can have home-cooked baby food always on hand if you make a large quantity of purée in advance, and freeze spoonfuls of it in a sterilized ice-cube tray.

NUTRITION AT THE READY
When frozen, turn the cubes of puréed food out of the tray and store in sealed freezer bags, one type of food per bag. Carefully label and date each bag and use within three months of freezing.

Freezing and storing

At this stage your baby is only tasting a tiny amount of food. Unused purée can be spooned into a sterilized ice-cube tray and frozen until needed. You can also freeze ahead – make a large amount of purée, spoon it into a sterilized ice-cube tray and freeze until the cubes are solid. Turn the cubes into a plastic bag, seal and label before returning to the freezer. Individual cubes can then be removed and defrosted in the fridge in a bowl or on a plate. Heat through as and when required.

You can sterilize a freshly washed ice-cube tray by washing it in the dishwasher or putting it in a pan of boiling water for five to 10 minutes.

Food hygiene

Food poisoning is easy to prevent. Make eating safe for your baby by taking the following precautions:

★ wash your hands carefully before feeding your baby – especially if you have been handling raw food

★ keep kitchen equipment and work spaces as clean as possible

★ don't save leftovers from the bowl your baby has just used – bacteria will grow and any enzymes from your baby's saliva will thin the food out

★ if you are using a ready-made jar of food, remove as much as you need rather than feeding directly from the jar, unless you are finishing the jar off

★ if you are heating your baby's food, heat only enough for one meal and discard any leftovers

★ keep food cold in the fridge for up to 24 hours and use warm food as soon as it's ready.

" Bethany turned her nose up at baby rice but she **seems to like** puréed carrot. Next week I'll introduce some **new vegetables** – I don't want her getting bored! "

DEBBIE is mum to six-month-old Bethany

3

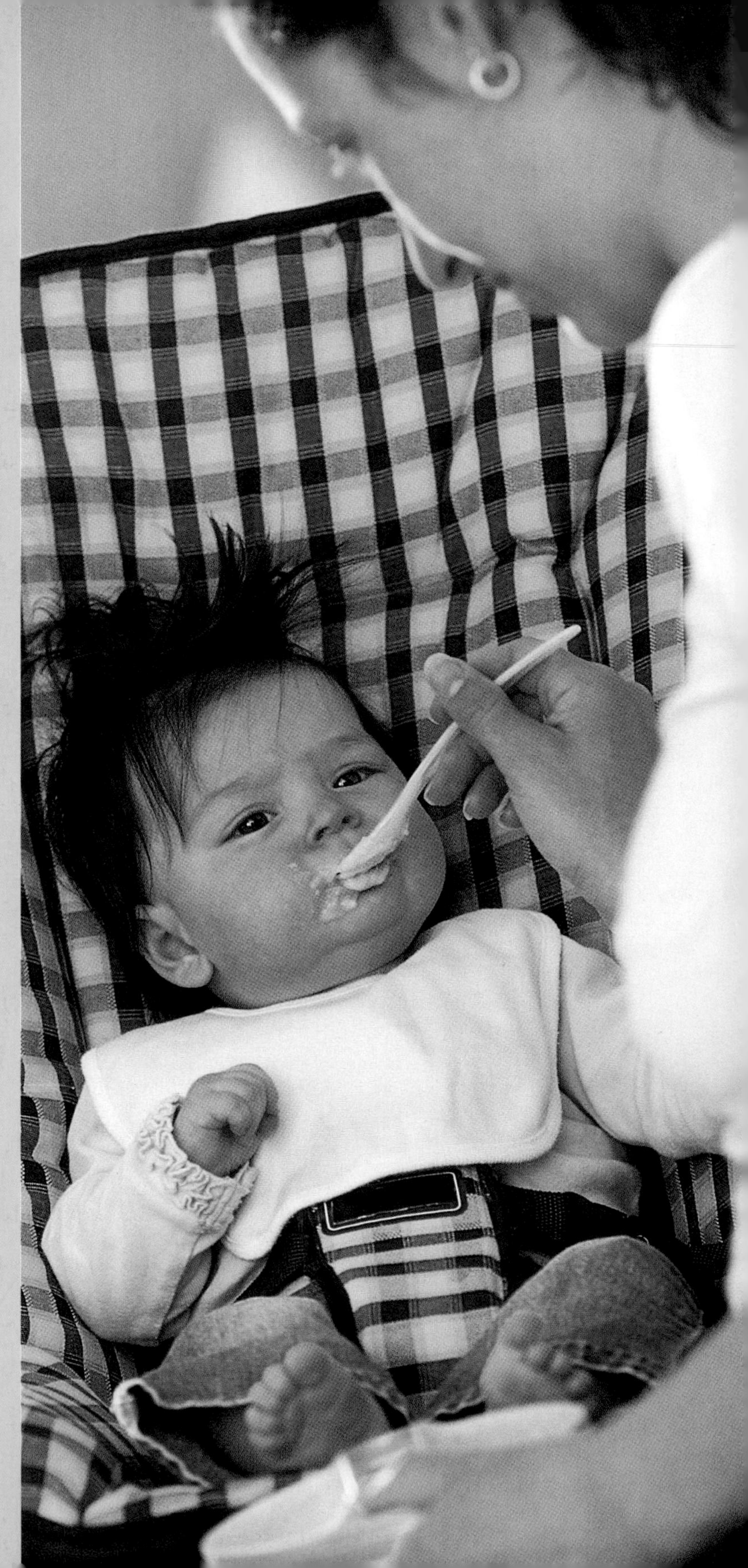

Around 6 months

Some time around her six-month birthday you can give your baby her first taste of solid food. She may start on baby rice or carrot purée. If she likes it you can start to introduce new foods and food combinations, helping her build up to two or three mini-meals a day. Don't expect too much too soon – your baby will take time to adjust to her new eating routine.

A happy routine

If your baby loves her first tastes, over the next few weeks you can start introducing a wider variety, but it's important to take your time, and watch out for allergic reactions.

Keep to the same routine each time you offer your baby some food. Establishing consistent, predictable mealtimes at this early age will help your baby become aware of what is happening – and what is expected of her. Always chat to her about what you are doing, talk about the food and utensils, smile and tell her how well she is doing.

Introducing new foods

For a healthy diet your baby ideally needs to eat as wide a range of foods as possible. Once she is eating two or three spoonfuls of baby cereal or a home-made purée such as carrot every day, try a different single food. Don't be worried if she doesn't accept it straight away. It's perfectly normal to have to offer a new food between 10 and 20 times before it's accepted. Once your baby clearly likes the taste, give this new food exclusively for at least a couple of days before trying another.

Offering one food at a time, and only one new food every two or three days, has two advantages:

- your baby can get used to each new taste and texture
- if there are any signs of an allergic reaction – such as tummy ache, diarrhoea or rashes – you will more readily identify which food was the culprit.

First purées (see pages 14–15) to try include:

- **vegetables:** carrot, parsnip, swede, potato, sweet potato

Expert tip

The number of "meals" your baby will have each day will depend on your baby. To begin with, solid food is just an addition to her diet and not a replacement for the breast milk or formula she needs. If after a few days she's just managing a couple of teaspoons once a day, that's fine. If she gives you the impression she'd like more, you can offer her the same size serving twice or even three times a day.

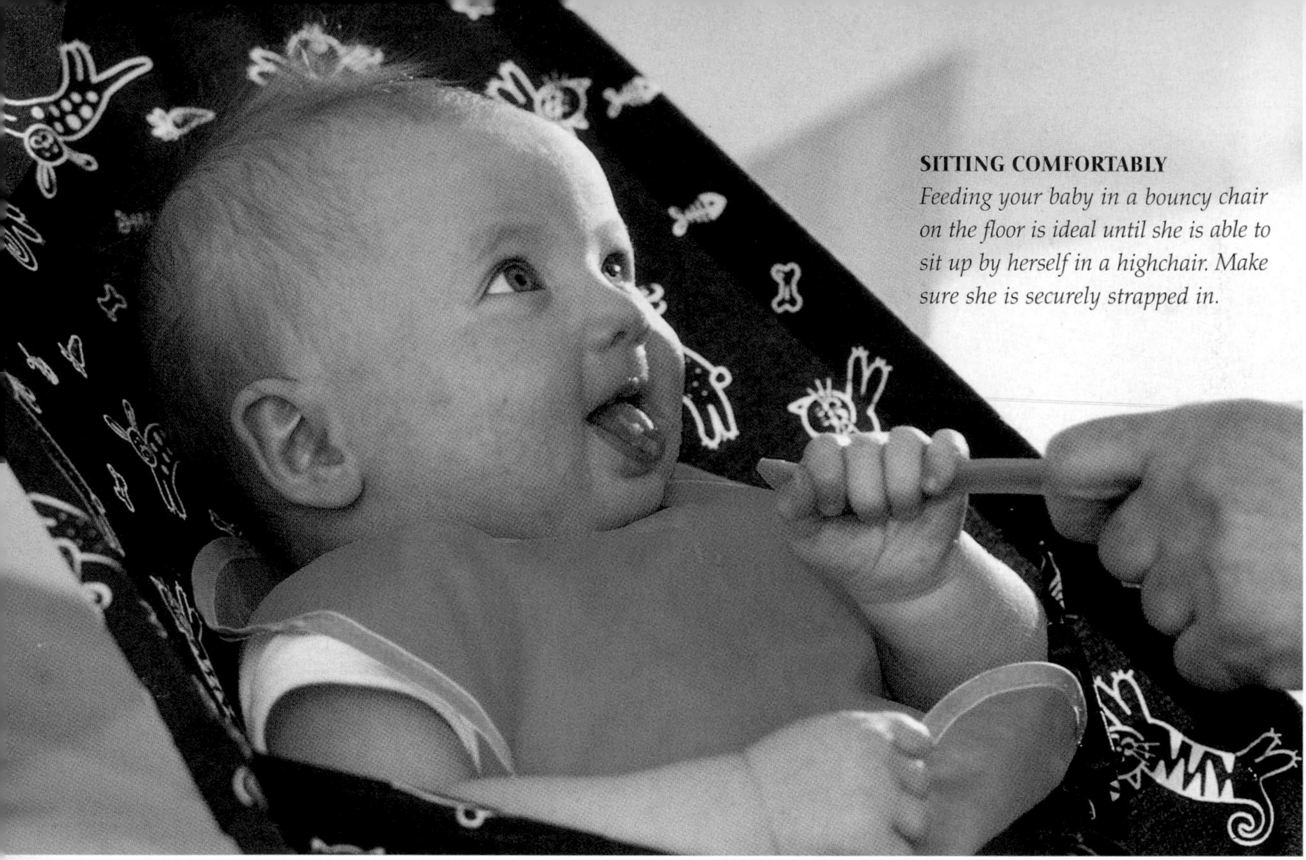

SITTING COMFORTABLY
Feeding your baby in a bouncy chair on the floor is ideal until she is able to sit up by herself in a highchair. Make sure she is securely strapped in.

"I prepare Daniel's purée before giving him a breastfeed. He loves sitting in his chair watching me. I'm sure he's finishing on the breast quicker so he can get to his solid food sooner!"

SIMONE is mum to Daniel, six months

- **fruit:** cooked apple, cooked pear, mashed banana, mango, melon, peach, avocado.

Once your baby is happy taking semi-liquid food from a spoon, gradually start to thicken the purée or cereal by adding less liquid. This allows your baby to practise her chewing (gumming) and swallowing skills and will help ease the transition from purées to lumpier food.

If your baby has a reaction

Although some foods are more likely than others to cause problems, any food can potentially trigger an allergic reaction. Food allergies that affect the immune system are rare, but some children find certain foods more difficult to tolerate than others and may have a reaction.

If you think your baby had a reaction to a particular food, wait a couple of weeks before trying it again. The same reaction two or three times would suggest that your baby is sensitive and you should wait a few months before re-introducing it. Most babies eventually grow out of this kind of food problem. Consult your health visitor if you are unsure.

Food combinations

Once your baby has taken several single foods with no adverse reaction you can start mixing two foods

together. Don't be tempted to try mixing one food your baby loves with another she hates, as she may end up hating both. Combinations that work well at this age include:

- broccoli and sweet potato
- carrot and parsnip
- potato and parsnip
- stewed apple and pear
- banana and mango
- melon and peach.

Does she like it?

Sometimes it can be difficult to tell from your baby's reaction whether or not she likes the new food on offer. Sweet foods such as mashed banana or stewed apple are usually accepted with a look of real pleasure. But if your baby screws up her face or even appears to wince, this doesn't necessarily mean she doesn't like what she's eating.

Remember every new taste will be unfamiliar if a baby's only experience of food up until now has been milk. Your baby's facial expression may just be a reaction to the new taste or texture. Offer her another taste – if she opens her mouth she obviously wants to try it again. If she turns her head away don't persist, but don't give up altogether either. Try it again a few

Milk needs

Once your baby is happily taking two or three solid "meals" a day (although these meals may consist of only a couple of spoonfuls at each serving) with milk in between, you may find that she's not feeding as much from the breast or bottle. Usually, the early morning and pre-bedtime feed stay the same, but during the day your baby may nurse a little less or take a little less formula.

- **Good for nutrition** Although your baby is starting to eat real food, milk is still an essential part of her diet. Purées offer little in the way of extra calories – and calories are what your baby needs to maintain her growth and weight gain. Until she's on three proper meals a day, she still needs around 600ml (20fl oz) of milk a day. If you are breastfeeding it's impossible to check, but if you let your baby take the lead chances are she's taking what she needs. If you have concerns, talk to your health visitor.

- **Good for comfort** Although your baby is starting to recognize that solids can satisfy hunger as well as milk, sucking is still a way of feeling close to you. Your baby loves nothing better than feeling safe and secure in your arms, and breastfeeding or bottle-feeding her is still important as a way of giving her comfort.

Tummy complaints

- If your baby becomes constipated, avoid baby cereals for a while and offer her fruit or vegetable purées and plenty of fluids such as breast milk, formula or cooled, boiled water.
- If your baby has a bout of diarrhoea, avoid the food she last had for a while – it may be that she cannot digest that particular food yet. Try again in a few weeks' time.
- Changes in diet may cause upset to your baby's tummy. Speak to your doctor or health visitor if you have any worries about your baby's reaction to food.

days later – but don't look anxious or concerned when you offer it. You don't want to unconsciously influence your baby's reaction.

Your baby's appetite

It's normal for your baby's appetite to vary from day to day. One day she'll amaze you by how much she eats and the next day she will frustrate you because she won't want a thing!

Changes in appetite can be caused by lots of different factors, including a growth spurt, how tired or alert your baby feels, whether she's unwell, and even the weather. The cold, for example, makes food taste different, and so can feeling cross. For these reasons, the foods that yesterday she loved may today be less appealing. It's also natural for your baby to develop preferences – for example, some children, because of genetic influences, are more able to distinguish bitter taste, and some prefer strong flavours, others sweet.

Developing good habits

Encouraging your baby to develop good eating habits now will have a positive effect on her health and wellbeing throughout her life.

- Getting her used to lots of different tastes now will help her enjoy a varied diet later – once she's eaten a new food for two or three days without difficulty, introduce another.

Questions & Answers

My baby will eat only puréed fruit. How can I encourage her to try vegetable purées?
Babies often show their dislike for food which isn't sweet. This is because they are used to breast milk or formula, both of which are quite sweet. Try thinning a vegetable purée with her usual milk – this may encourage her to give it a go. She may also find carrot and sweet potato more palatable than green vegetables.

By the time she's finished her milk feed my baby isn't hungry. How can I improve her appetite?
Your baby is probably too full after her milk to bother with solid food. Cut down on the amount of breast milk she has before a solid feed – just give her enough to take the edge off her appetite. Then offer her the remainder of her milk feed after her solids.

My baby doesn't appear to swallow anything – most of what I put in her mouth comes straight out again! What can I do about this?
If your baby consistently pushes her food out with her tongue so it dribbles down her chin it may be too thick for her to handle. Remember, until now she's only had food the consistency of water. Try diluting her food more – and use a bib to help save on the washing.

My baby often cries for her food – and then carries on crying between mouthfuls. Why does she do this?
Your baby is used to sucking when she's hungry – and it will take her a while before she realizes that solid food will satisfy her in the way that milk does. If she takes the food willingly but continues to cry while eating, this doesn't necessarily mean she doesn't like what you are giving her – it may just mean that she's still hungry.

BABY KNOWS BEST
Offer your baby small amounts of purée on a sterilized spoon. Go at her pace and remember that her appetite may change from day to day.

- Avoid adding sugar or salt to her food – not only are they bad for her health in general, salt can damage her kidneys. Also, once children get used to these tastes, food that's less highly seasoned can seem bland. You can use a tiny amount of herbs for seasoning.
- Give your baby lots of attention at mealtimes – chat to her, stroke her hair and praise her for eating well.
- Encourage your baby to join in – she's a long way off being able to feed herself but she'll enjoy having her own spoon to wave around.
- Make feeding a family affair – moving on to solids is a great way for dad to get involved too, especially if until now you have only breastfed.

Messy eaters

Even though you have control over the spoon, don't expect to be able to keep your baby – or your kitchen – spotless. First foods are as much about experimenting as nourishment – and your baby will be desperate to get her hands on the spoon and the dish. As your baby needs lots of positive attention it's best to try to ignore the inevitable mess by:

- keeping lots of kitchen towels on hand for wiping up
- always putting a washable bib on your baby before each mealtime
- spreading a mess mat or newspaper on the floor under her baby chair
- keeping a rubbish bag to hand.

Shop-bought baby food

There are lots of advantages to making your own baby food – it's cheap, easy and your baby can get

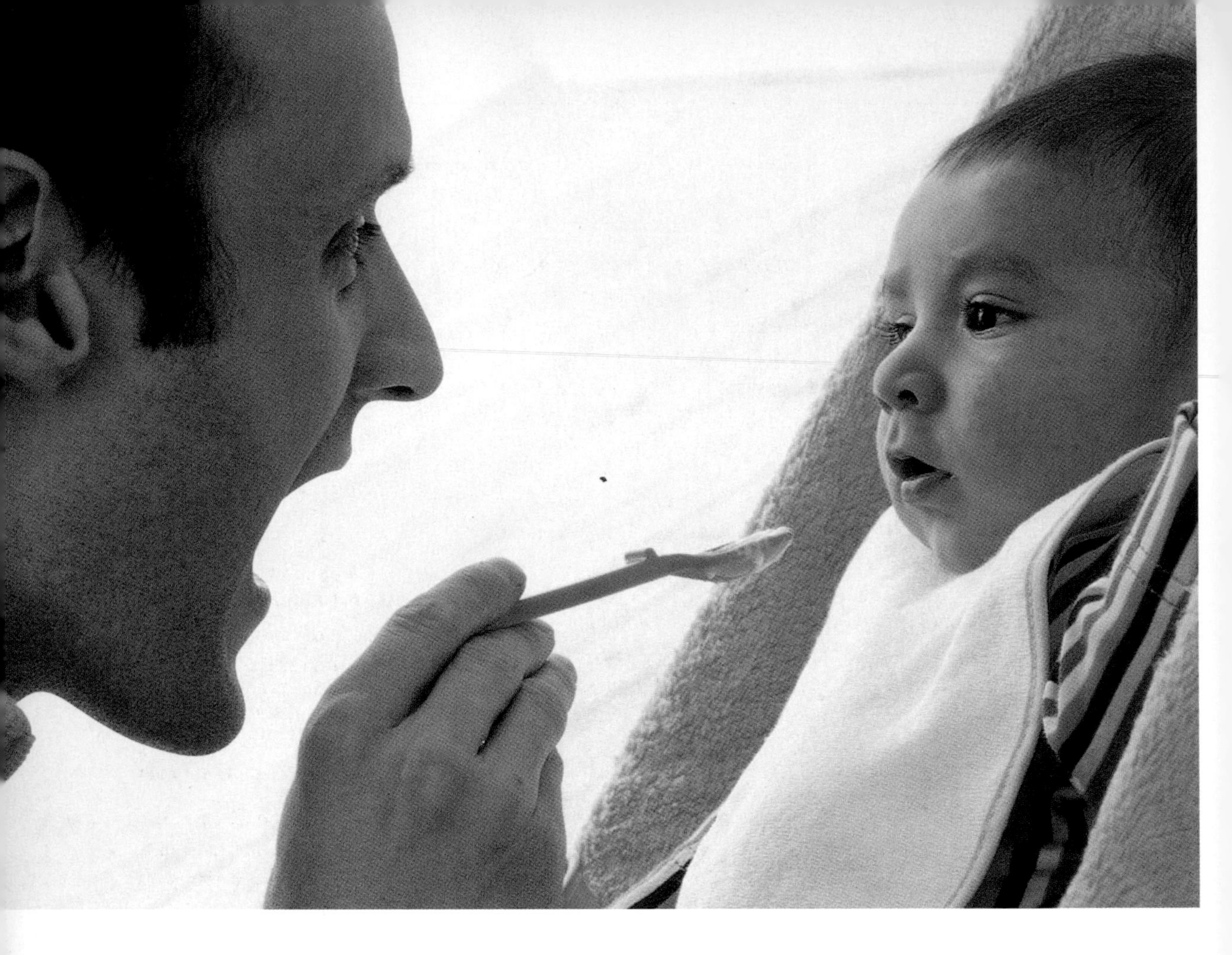

WATCH AND LEARN
Open your mouth as you offer your baby her food, and she will probably open hers in response.

What is gluten?

Gluten is a protein that's found in wheat, barley, rye and perhaps oats. Sensitivity to gluten can trigger coeliac disease (see page 54). In a small number of babies, when the intestine comes into contact with gluten an allergic reaction occurs in its lining. The lining becomes smooth, preventing nutrients from being properly absorbed, and this is associated with a permanent intolerance to gluten. Symptoms include tummy pain, diarrhoea, weight loss, irritability and nausea.

Foods that contain gluten, such as bread, pasta, and rusks, should never be given to babies under six months. Once your baby is six months old, her gut is more mature and less susceptible to developing gluten intolerance.

If coeliac disease is diagnosed, your child will need to eat a gluten-free diet for life. She'll be referred to a dietician who can advise you as to what she can and can't eat. Nowadays, larger supermarkets stock gluten-free alternatives, including bread, biscuits, cereals and pasta.

used to the types of food your family normally eats. But there are times when ready-made jars are more convenient – when you are travelling is a good example.

You can choose from lots of different flavours and ingredients and they are usually categorized according to age. They don't contain salt but some do have added sugar and modified starch, so it's worth reading the list of ingredients carefully.

When using commercially made baby food, keep your baby safe by following these guides:

- check the use-by date on the container
- store unopened jars in a cool place
- make sure the vacuum seal button is down – don't use a jar if the seal has popped up
- don't feed from the jar – take the amount of food your baby needs out of the jar and serve separately
- once opened, keep the jar with its remaining contents in the fridge – it should stay fresh for one to two days, but always read the label.

Foods to avoid

Advice on which foods are suitable for your baby can sometimes change, so check also with a health visitor or at your baby clinic. But as a general guideline you should not give the following foods to babies who are six months old:

- **nuts and nut products**, especially those containing peanuts: for babies with a family history of allergies continue to avoid these up to the age of three; whole nuts should not be given to children until age seven or older because of the risk of choking
- **foods that carry a higher risk of food poisoning** such as mould-ripened cheeses, liver pâté and soft-boiled eggs (up to the age of nine months only yolk should be given as this is the high-nutrition part of an egg, and whites are more likely to cause allergies)
- **salt**: your baby's kidneys are too immature to cope with this
- **sugar, honey or other sweeteners**: can lead to a sweet tooth and honey can also contain a potentially dangerous spore (see page 18) – if you need to, sweeten desserts with mashed banana
- **soft drinks**: may contain high levels of artificial sweeteners; offer cooled, boiled water or occasionally diluted unsweetened fruit juice at mealtimes if you want to give your baby an alternative to milk
- **tea**: can reduce iron absorption
- **low-fat and high-fibre foods**: babies need more calories and less bulk to give them the energy they need to grow
- **processed foods**: these contain too much salt.

Are organic fruit and vegetables best?

Many people are worried about the effects on children's health of pesticides and other chemicals used to produce food. Organic fruit and vegetables are grown in soil fertilized with manure and compost rather than synthetic chemicals. Research has shown, however, that levels of pesticide in produce such as fruit and vegetables are typically well below the safety levels set by government agencies. You can take extra care with your child's health by washing fruit and vegetables thoroughly before cooking and serving.

Every baby is different

Your baby may take a couple of weeks to get the hang of solids. This is fine, as long as she is drinking plenty of milk to meet her nutritional needs.

On the other hand, your baby may race ahead and manage two or three "meals" a day in no time at all. If your baby is happily eating solids, coping well with taking food from a spoon, and enjoying a wide range of fruit and vegetable purées, you may wish gradually to start introducing other foods such as meat, poultry, lentils or split peas to her purées.

Remember that your baby's digestive system is still adjusting to solid food, so add only small quantities of new foods – and still just one at a time in case she has an allergic reaction. You may find it takes longer for your baby to accept meat and poultry, so purée a tiny amount with her favourite vegetable.

"Not all of Rowan's food ends up in his mouth – especially when he tries to **feed himself**! But he's having such a good time, I just **don't worry** about the mess."

STEPHANIE is mum to Rowan, seven months

4

7 to 9 months

Your baby is growing up quickly and mealtimes are becoming a very different affair. In the next few weeks he'll learn how to chew and will discover the fun of finger foods. Now he can sit up on his own you can invest in a highchair. And, as the number of foods you can give your baby rapidly expands, mealtimes will become easier as he starts to enjoy some of the same foods as everyone else.

Gaining independence

Over the next few months your baby will be building up to three regular meals a day with two or three snacks in between. While you prepare his meals, remember to keep chatting to him about his food, what you are doing and how well he is doing. Make sure you keep distractions such as television and toys well out of sight.

He'll now be sitting up on his own for extended periods and he'll be keen to get more involved in feeding himself. Letting him have a spoon of his own will encourage him - as will offering him finger foods. Invest in plenty of bibs and a mess mat! Playing with food - touching it, pulling it apart, even throwing it - is perfectly normal.

It's best not to worry about how much ends up on the floor and how much food actually reaches his mouth. Your baby will eat when he's hungry, and your role is to keep mealtimes as happy and relaxed as possible.

Introducing more texture

The range of foods your baby can eat will gradually increase (see page 37) and you can start introducing lumpier food so he can develop his chewing skills. He'll still use his gums to chew for a while yet so don't imagine he'll be able to cope with a steak - even if his first teeth have appeared! Instead, mash rather than purée his meals using a fork or potato masher. Softer food that's suitable for eating with fingers, such as bread or pasta, can be left whole.

Talk to your health visitor if your baby does not seem to accept foods that are more textured.

Expert tips

As your baby naturally becomes more inquisitive and active you'll need to be extra alert and take precautions to help keep him safe.

- Do always strap your baby into his highchair – between seven and nine months is an age when he is mastering lots of new physical skills and may try to climb out. This is especially dangerous if he should fall with food in his mouth as he could choke.
- Don't let your baby eat anything he's already mouthed and then left lying around for an hour or so – it may give him a tummy upset.
- Do always supervise your baby when he is eating or drinking – almost all children gag on some food at some stage and you need to be close by to react quickly if this happens (see page 34).

When is the best time to start giving my baby finger foods?

Every day your baby is getting better at using his hands and fingers and this makes it easier for him to do things such as trying to feed himself. His hand-eye coordination is coming on in leaps and bounds, and now he can pick up a piece of food and then put it into his mouth - although not without a bit of mess!

"I CAN HOLD IT" *Your baby will be triumphant as she masters the ability to pick up pieces of food herself and put them in her mouth.*

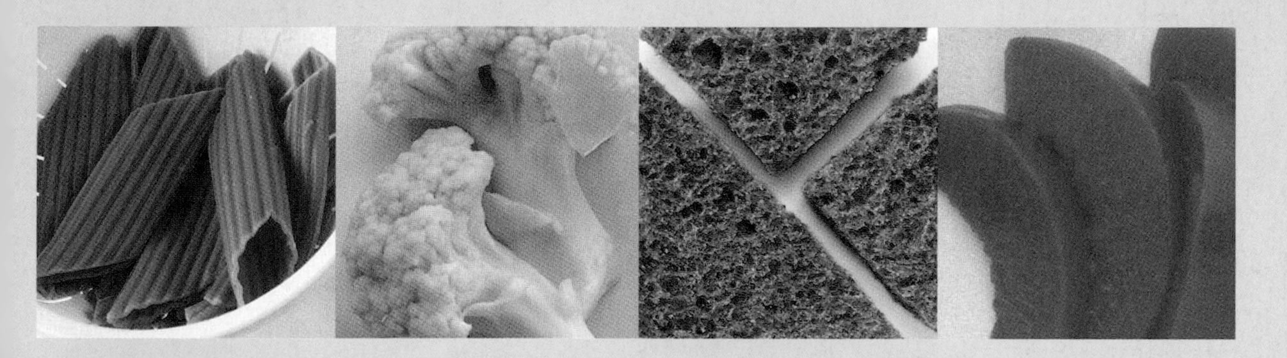

Getting started

Most babies are ready for finger food by about seven months. For a while yet, your baby will hold the food in his fist and work hard to push in the last mouthful using the flat of his hand. Over the next few months, however, he'll start to pick up things using his thumb and forefinger, a skill called the pincer grasp. In time this will allow him to pick up tiny pieces of food such as raisins or peas.

Your baby can easily choke by eating too fast or putting too much into his mouth. Stay close – and never leave your baby alone at mealtimes.

Learning to chew

Practising chewing is important not just because it means your baby can eat a wider range of food. Chewing also helps your baby practise moving his mouth and tongue, ready to learn how to talk. Your baby is using his gums to chew so choose foods that can be gummed to a soft consistency for swallowing or those that will dissolve in his mouth without chewing. Here are some ideas:

★ cubes of bread, rice cakes and toast

★ dry cereals

★ chunks of soft fruit such as banana or melon

★ small pieces of cooked vegetable such as carrot, broccoli and cauliflower

★ well-cooked pasta, cut down in size if necessary

★ tiny cubes of hard cheese.

PREPARING FINGER FOOD

Even if your baby has some teeth he'll still use his gums to chew for a while yet. Always cut food into manageable chunks and don't offer him too much at a time. He might just try and stuff it all in at once – or sweep the lot on to the floor!

Give your baby lots of encouragement:

- enthuse about each meal – offer him a spoonful with "Mmm, doesn't this look delicious?"
- offer familiar foods you know he likes – he's more likely to accept a coarser texture in a food he's enjoyed before
- avoid surprises – coming across a lump in a "smooth" food, such as fruit pulp in yogurt, may be upsetting and make him suspicious of other foods
- let him snack on finger foods – offering small cubes of toast or soft fruit between meals will allow him to discover new textures at his own pace.

MAKE MEALTIMES FUN
Keeping mealtimes relaxed and simply enjoying feeding your baby will ensure they become a fun part of your routine.

Preventing choking

Introducing lumpier food and finger food brings with it the risk of choking. Children don't learn to chew and swallow efficiently until they are two or three years old. And when they are first learning to eat finger food, they may bite off large pieces and try to swallow it without chewing first. If your baby starts to gag or choke on a piece of food – or anything else – he may not be able to cough forcefully enough to dislodge it without help.

Minimize the risk of choking by:

- staying with him at all times while he is eating
- cutting his food into pieces small enough to swallow whole
- encouraging him to eat slowly and not gulp his food
- only letting him eat when he's sitting down – not running around or playing
- teaching him to chew and swallow first before talking or laughing
- always harnessing him into his highchair – if he falls out with food in his mouth he may choke
- never giving him the following:
  - large pieces of raw carrot
  - whole grapes
  - popcorn
  - uncooked peas
  - celery
  - hard sweets

Take care also with hot dogs and other types of meat sticks – they should always be cut lengthways and then into smaller pieces.

Meal ideas

- **Breakfast**

Rice cakes; well-cooked scrambled egg yolk; mashed banana; wholemeal toast fingers; breakfast cereal (made up with whole cow's milk) with fruit purée.

- **Lunch/tea**

Mashed vegetables and minced chicken; cauliflower cheese with carrot; pasta with tomato sauce and grated cheese; boned white fish with well-cooked rice and peas; shepherd's pie.

- **Puddings**

Natural yogurt with fruit purée; pear slices (skin and pips removed); home-made rice pudding with finely chopped dried apricots.

Choosing a highchair

A highchair will keep your baby safe, provide a seat at the right height, and you can use it between meals for your baby to sit in and play with his toys. Look for:

- sturdy construction – folding models are often the most popular as they collapse for easy storage
- a five-point safety harness – you should always strap your baby into his highchair, even if he'll be sitting in it for only a few minutes
- a good-size food/play tray that's easy to clean; a deep rim will help prevent dishes and food being pushed off and a detachable tray will help with cleaning
- a wipe-clean comfortable padded seat.

Questions & Answers

My baby won't eat. How can I encourage him?

There will be times when your baby either rejects his food outright or is more inclined to play with it than eat it. At this age babies are easily distracted – so it's worth making sure mealtimes take place at quiet times of the day when you can give him your full attention. If he's only interested in playing with his food, he's probably just not hungry. It may also be the case that your baby is teething – first teeth usually make an appearance between six and nine months, and it's not unusual for babies to go off eating if they are suffering from teething pain or discomfort. Never force your child to eat and avoid making mealtimes a battle. If he doesn't want any more, take his food away and try again later with something else.

We make a terrible mess every mealtime! How can I stop my baby from trying to grab the spoon from me?

Babies like to imitate and if your baby sees you with a spoon he'll want one too. Satisfy his need for independence by giving him his own spoon to hold but make sure he's getting enough food by still using one yourself and slipping in mouthfuls when you can. And meanwhile, try to ignore the mess – this phase will soon pass!

My baby spits out lumps. What should I do?

If this happens, don't rush your baby – until now he's known only how to suck and learning to chew and cope with more lumpy food requires a very different technique. Make sure he has plenty of opportunities to practise chewing by offering him finger foods as soon as he can hold them and keep offering him lumpy food.

FROM BOTTLE TO BEAKER
Drinking from a cup rather than a bottle is better for your baby's teeth and speech development.

Foods to avoid

At this age there are still certain foods that are not suitable for your baby. Continue to avoid:

- **adding salt, sugar and honey**: use mashed banana for sweetening desserts instead
- **nuts**: avoid all nuts and nut products, especially if your family is known to have a history of allergies
- **foods that present a choking hazard**: these include whole grapes, nuts, large pieces of apple or raw carrot, uncooked peas and celery
- **soft drinks**: may contain high levels of artificial sweeteners; offer cooled, boiled water and occasionally diluted fruit juice at mealtimes if you want an alternative to milk
- **foods that carry a higher risk of food poisoning** such as mould-ripened cheeses, liver pâté and soft-boiled eggs (up to the age of nine months only yolk should be given as this is the high-nutrition part of an egg, and whites are more likely to cause allergies)
- **low-fat and high-fibre foods**: babies need more calories and less bulk to give them the energy they need to grow
- **processed foods**: these contain too much salt.

Advancing to a cup

Your baby will naturally feel thirsty while he's eating. This is a good time to introduce a beaker or cup so he can take sips of water or fruit juice during mealtimes. Limit the amount of juice he drinks to 120ml (4fl oz) a day and dilute it at least one part juice to three parts water.

- Choose a non-drip, soft-spout cup for first-timers. Some babies prefer a cup with one or two handles, others prefer no handles – you may need to experiment.
- Help by holding the cup to your baby's mouth and tipping it for him to show him how it works.

Milk needs

Your baby still needs lots of calories every day for energy and growth. Introducing a wider variety of food into his diet – especially protein and dairy foods – helps a lot. But to make sure your baby is getting enough protein, calcium and vitamins, whatever else he eats, he still needs about 500–600ml (17–20fl oz) of formula or two full breastfeeds every day.

- Expect your baby just to play with it at first – chances are it will be waved around and thrown from the highchair. Playing with it is all part of the learning process.
- Avoid letting him carry it around with him – offer it to him only while he is in his highchair.

Extra value foods

- **Mashed bananas**

These are a high-energy food and can be easily digested. They are also full of nutrients, such as vitamins B and C, potassium, magnesium and iodine.

- **Finely chopped meat**

Beef and lamb, in particular, are rich sources of iron and zinc.

- **Vitamin C** (in fruit and vegetables or diluted fruit juice)

Helps aid iron absorption when served at the same time as iron-rich foods.

Foods your baby can eat

Your baby is now ready for a whole range of tastes and can share many of your family meals – provided no sugar or salt has been added. Remember to introduce new tastes and textures gradually.

Try to include at least one protein-based meal a day – fish, meat, egg yolks, lentils or beans – as these are good sources of protein and iron. Iron is particularly important as by the time your baby is six months old the iron stores with which he was born are starting to dwindle and milk alone will not satisfy all his daily requirements (see page 7).

Make sure your baby also has a portion of fruit, vegetables and starchy food every day, too. He can also eat foods containing gluten, so try white or wholemeal bread, pasta or couscous.

And you can now use cow's milk in meals – added to cereal, for example.

Protein

- beans and pulses
- cheese
- chicken/turkey
- cow's milk in meals (e.g. with cereal)
- eggs (yolks only, as their nutritional value is higher and they are less likely to cause allergies than whites)
- boneless fish
- red meat
- tofu

Fruit

- grapes (cut in half and pips removed)
- orange (seedless)
- mango
- melon
- satsuma
- strawberries
- pieces of pear

Vegetables

- butternut squash
- cucumber
- green beans
- leek
- peas
- mushroom
- onion
- sweetcorn

Starchy food

- potatoes
- bread
- noodles
- rice
- pasta
- couscous
- breakfast cereals
- porridge

" Feeding Nicola is **much simpler** now. I just take a little out of our main meal – potato, vegetables and meat – and mash it up for her. It's **better than ready-made** any day. "

CAROLINE is mum to Nicola, nine months

5

9 to 12 months

Your baby's personality is starting to shine through, and as her sense of self grows, so does her desire for independence. Over the next few months she'll work hard at learning how to feed herself and with your patience and praise she'll soon master this essential skill. Meanwhile, you can enjoy her company at the table – this is a great time to start letting her join in with family meals.

Advancing skills

Your baby now has regular mealtimes with three meals – breakfast, lunch and tea – every day and two or three snacks as well. She can cope well with mashed or chopped food and uses finger foods to practise her chewing skills. There is now little she can't eat, so family meals can be easily adapted to feed your baby too. Carry on talking to her about what you are doing when you are preparing the meals and give her lots of praise.

Your baby's new skills make mealtimes easier:

- she can now chew; cope with different textures; and pick up shapes – talk to your health visitor if she is having difficulties with any of these
- her hand-eye coordination is developing fast and learning how to feed herself is a natural step towards independence
- she's starting to recognize lots of familiar words such as "beaker" and "lunchtime"
- she loves interacting with people and will enjoy social get-togethers such as mealtimes.

Introducing new tastes

Your older baby is becoming much more active – learning to crawl and then walk – which means she needs extra calories for energy and growth. She also needs a wide variety of nutrients in her diet so now is a good time to introduce her to a broader range of foods. As her natural inclination is to explore everything she can get her hands on – including food – this is a great age to offer your baby new tastes, although as she enjoys some independence, she is also beginning to show clear food preferences.

Extra equipment

You will find the following useful as your baby becomes more experienced at feeding herself:

- **plastic feeding bowl** with a suction pad to prevent her flinging food all over the floor
- **plastic bib** with a moulded tray to catch the food that doesn't make it into her mouth
- **portable highchair** that screws or clips onto a table top – a great help when you are out visiting friends or relatives or on holiday.

Encouraging self-feeding

Your baby is developing a strong sense of herself in the family and of her daily routines. She'll start to look forward to mealtimes, and will recognize the cues that mean food is on the way. She'll also want to be just like you – which means feeding herself, rather than being fed by you. Encouraging your baby to self-feed means that, for a while at least, mealtimes will take longer and be messier. To begin with, your baby will probably keep turning over the spoon before it reaches her mouth. But as her finger and hand skills develop she'll soon master the art of feeding herself.

Help her reach this milestone by:

- giving her lots of chances to practise – and ignoring the mess!
- making sure she's getting enough food in her mouth by helping her load her spoon and slipping in mouthfuls with your own spoon in between attempts
- serving her food that will stay on the spoon more easily – mashed potato with cheese, thick yogurts and fromage frais, for example
- resisting the temptation to take over – letting her have a go, and eventually succeed, will do wonders for her confidence.

Talk to your health visitor if your child shows no interest in self-feeding.

Getting the portions right

Every baby's appetite is different – and can change from day to day. This means it can be hard to judge how much food your baby needs. Remember that a baby's stomach can't hold very much and therefore she'll need to eat more frequently than you.

It's good to encourage your baby to feed at regular times but accept also that your baby will probably need a snack in between mealtimes to help fill the gaps. When she's uninterested, let her out of her highchair after 10 minutes or so and offer her another meal or snack a couple of hours later.

Teething and eating

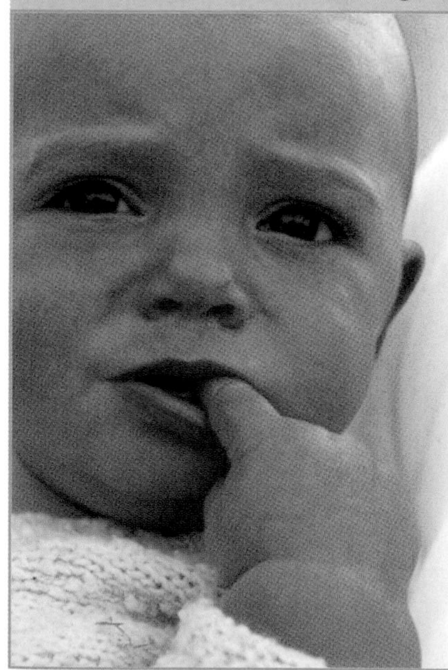

When your baby is teething don't be surprised if she goes off her food. Over the next couple of months she'll have lots of teeth coming through and, although some babies take teething in their stride and show no ill-effects, others become fretful and irritable.

The common signs of teething include swollen, reddened gums, excessive drooling, an inflamed cheek, mild cough and even a low-grade fever. Your baby will also want to bite down on anything she can get in her mouth.

If pain and discomfort affect your baby's appetite she'll need more milk for a while. She may also refuse to drink from a beaker, despite having previously loved the independence it gave her. Bottle-feeding your baby again shouldn't be a problem as long as it's only short term.

Meanwhile, chewing and sucking on firm-textured finger food that becomes soft for easy swallowing can help soothe your baby's gums – and offer her some extra nutrition at the same time. You could also try, for example, a frozen banana or chilled wholemeal crust. But never leave her alone with food in case she chokes. Commercially made teething biscuits are best avoided as they contain a lot of sugar. Cold food – such as chilled puréed apple – may also be more appealing than warm food.

INDEPENDENT FEEDING
The time will come when your baby wants her independence. Allowing her to feed herself will boost her confidence and she will quickly master the skills she needs.

Don't allow your child to carry a bottle or food around between meals or snacks as this will lessen her appetite, and a family rule of no food between meals will increase the likelihood of her eating more at mealtimes.

Planning her meals

Your baby should have at least one daily portion of fish, meat, egg, lentils or beans (these are the best sources of protein and iron) as well as food from the four main food groups every day. These groups are:

- dairy products such as cheese, yogurt or full-fat fromage frais (don't rely on just cheese for protein – use meat, fish or egg yolks, too)
- starchy foods such as potatoes, bread, noodles, rice, pasta, couscous and breakfast cereals
- fruit and vegetables: offer a selection of fresh fruit and vegetables so she gets used to different tastes and textures

Expert tip

Your baby can now eat the same food as you as long as it doesn't contain added salt, sugar or honey (see page 18). You should also avoid giving her:

- foods that carry a high risk of food poisoning (such as mould-ripened cheese, liver pâté and soft-boiled eggs)
- whole nuts (ground nuts are fine, unless there is a history of allergies in which case you should avoid all nuts).

When can my baby join in family meals?

Now is a great time for your baby to join in with family meals. She's a little individual with a real personality and she enjoys having fun with everyone. Her ability to understand language is coming on fast and she's really trying to communicate with you. Even if she doesn't have the same food, feeding your baby when the rest of the family is eating together has lots of benefits.

A FAMILY AFFAIR
Children who regularly eat meals with the family are less likely to be fussy eaters and more likely to try a wider range of foods.

It's good to eat together

Family mealtimes are about more than just making sure everyone is getting fed – they are also social occasions and great opportunities for your baby to learn about good table manners and conversation.

Eating with your baby will also make her more adventurous when it comes to food. A baby who won't eat green beans may change her mind when she sees everyone else enjoying them.

Keep the atmosphere light and easy going by:

★ planning family meals around your baby – if she's tired, eating together won't be fun for you or her

★ not expecting too much – if your baby turns her nose up at the food on her plate, don't take it personally, there could be various explanations for why she's not hungry today

★ ignoring the mess – have lots of paper towels handy for cleaning up as she goes.

• meat and meat alternatives such as soft, flaked white fish, well-chopped chicken or lamb and small quantities of well-cooked lentils or beans.

Babies' appetites are very changeable, however, so check your child's diet over a week rather than a day. Talk to your health visitor if you think she isn't eating all the foods she needs for good nutrition.

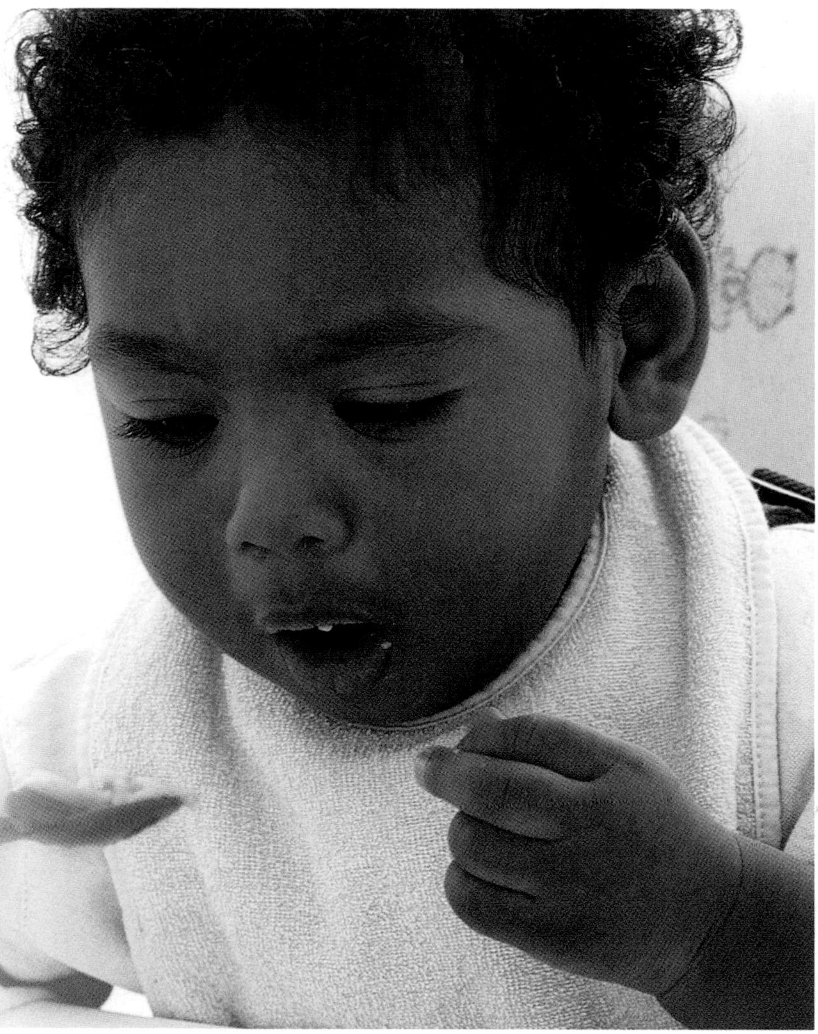

Meal ideas

• Breakfast

Yogurt smoothie and toast; porridge with dried fruit; Weetabix and milk with grated pear.

• Lunch/tea

Lasagne; sausages with mashed potato and vegetables; cut-up jacket potato with hummus/avocado/baked beans.

• Puddings

Baked bananas and full-fat plain yogurt; bread and butter pudding; wholemeal pancakes with fresh fruit; canned fruit in natural juice.

Questions & Answers

My baby is now nine months old and she still has no teeth. Should I be worried about this?

Many babies at nine months are still toothless – and some even make it to their first year without a single tooth in sight. Late teething needn't affect your baby's move onto chunkier food. Babies with and without teeth use their gums for chewing until their molars appear in the middle of the second year.

My baby doesn't seem to eat very much. Should I be encouraging her to eat more?

Your baby's tummy will fill up quickly on solid food so when she's had enough, don't insist she has one last mouthful. This may put her off the food she's eating as well as making her feel upset and resentful. Talk to your health visitor if your baby:

• tries to store food in her cheeks rather than swallow

• refuses to accept textured food.

Tips for healthy eating

One of the best ways you can help your baby to grow up fit and healthy is to help her develop healthy eating habits now. These guidelines will help.

- **If she rejects something today try again a few days later.**

Babies' tastes are notoriously fickle and just because she appears not to like something now there's no reason to assume she won't enjoy it another time. It can take 10–20 times of offering for a baby to accept a new food, and sometimes even longer.

- **Praise her when she eats well.**

Your baby will quickly realize that healthy, natural food is good for her if you tell her how clever she is when she eats it.

- **Avoid "sugary" treats.**

Sugar and sugary foods contain what is termed "empty calories" – lots of sugar and energy but little else of nutritional value.

- **Offer healthy snacks.**

It may be easier to reach for the biscuit tin when your baby is hungry between meals, but it's worth getting her used to nutritious snacks.

- **Don't allow your child to graze between meals.**

If your child sits in her highchair for a meal or snack every two to three hours she will not be hungry in between – don't allow her to carry food or drink around with her.

Milk needs

Your baby should still be having at least 500–600ml (17–20fl oz) of breast milk or formula a day (this is equivalent to about two breastfeeds). Around this age, however, she may start to wean herself off the breast.

Losing interest in sucking can happen if your baby is eating lots of solids and is good at using a beaker. It may, however, only be temporary. Perhaps your baby is teething, in which case sucking can put pressure on painful gums. Your baby is also curious about the world around her – and she may be easily distracted if people are in the room or the television is on. Feed her in a quiet room without distractions.

Meanwhile, check that your baby is getting her full milk quota by offering her formula in her beaker. If she doesn't like this, supplement her diet with plenty of full-fat yogurts and hard cheese.

- Avoid fast food.

Pizzas, chicken nuggets and chips are all high in fats and salt and may contain additives too. If your child eats these foods regularly she may have a greater risk of developing health problems as an adult.

Thirst quenchers

Your baby may still be resisting using a beaker but it's worth persisting. Drinking from a beaker is better for speech development and for her teeth.

Give your baby water between meals if she seems thirsty. During the summer when she is losing fluid through sweat, you should also offer her a drink of water a couple of times during the day. Don't make a habit of giving her juice too often – maximum of 120ml (4fl oz) a day – she'll love the sweeter taste and quickly refuse anything else. Too much fruit juice can cause diarrhoea, nappy rash and contribute to poor dental health.

Watch out, food about!

Your baby is now much more skilled with her hands. She has mastered the pincer grasp and can pick up anything she comes across using her thumb and forefinger. This means she can guide pieces of food into her mouth more accurately – so self-feeding is getting much less messy.

She's also figured out how to "let go" of things. Be prepared for lots of dropping and picking up games (she drops, you pick up). By the end of her first year she'll have discovered how to throw as well.

"I always make extra for Rashmi and then freeze it for meals the following week. This saves me time – and also makes me feel less frustrated if she doesn't eat much."

NAWSHEEN is mum to Rashmi, 11 months

"Yu-lin has always been a great eater – but at 20 months he **started refusing** everything I put in front of him. Sitting down with him and not overfilling his plate has **helped a lot.**"

JUNG is mum to Yu-lin, 20 months

One year onwards

As your baby passes his first birthday he'll become more skilled at feeding himself. He now needs to give up the bottle permanently and you may decide it's time to stop breastfeeding, too. Over the next few months your child will also have a surge of independence - and will love trying to get his way, especially at mealtimes!

Wilful ways

Over the coming year your child will pass many major milestones – he'll discover how to walk, for example, and may say his first words. At around 18 months he'll also have a real drive towards independence and will want his own way whenever possible. Food inevitably becomes a battleground. Continue to involve your child in his mealtime routine by chatting to him while you prepare his food, avoiding distractions such as television and toys, and making sure he's properly seated when eating.

Fuss-free eating

Mealtimes with toddlers can be challenging, but most behaviour – from food fads and refusing to eat to making a mess and not sitting at the table – is perfectly normal. Knowing what to expect can help a lot. So does staying unfazed. It is likely that your toddler is just exercising his will and the less wound-up you become the quicker he'll realize his behaviour isn't having an effect.

Now your toddler can decide what he will and won't eat you may worry more about his diet. Even though there will be times when your cooking has gone to waste, it's important to keep offering a healthy, varied diet. At this age he also needs regular snacks to keep up his energy levels.

The toddler years

As your easy-going baby turns into a challenging toddler, mealtimes can become a potential minefield. But it's important to realize that changing appetites, rejection of food and food fads are all perfectly normal at this age. Even so, you may long for the days when food meant simply spooning purées into your baby's open mouth! Understanding how your child is growing and developing will help you avoid battles over food.

Happy meals

Remember to keep the atmosphere at mealtimes calm and relaxed.

Don't

- get into a fight with your toddler – losing your temper will make him more determined not to eat
- make him sit there for hours
- offer him an after-meal treat

Do

- end the meal as soon as it is obvious he won't change his mind
- remember it won't harm him to miss a few meals
- offer him the same type of food another time if he has rejected something. It takes 10–20 times for a child to see, smell, touch and taste foods before accepting them.

At this stage your child is:

- using up lots of energy
- developing likes and dislikes
- growing more independent
- getting easily distracted.

NO, NO, NO!
Don't worry if your child refuses to eat something – with the toddler years come surges of independence.

To help him you can:

- offer two familiar foods with one new food
- boost his energy with healthy snacks (see below)
- accept that he won't like everything you give him, but continue to offer a wide choice so he doesn't become hooked on just a handful of foods
- help him feel as if he has some control over mealtimes by offering him food that he can easily feed himself and the chance to choose from, say, two different pieces of fruit for pudding
- sit down and eat with him whenever possible to help him enjoy his meals.

Successful mealtimes

There's little you can't give your one year old to eat, but that doesn't mean he'll love everything you put in front of him. Accept that, for a while yet, he'll still prefer certain tastes and textures. Try keeping to these general guidelines for mealtime success.

- **Simple cooking** Your child may not like cooked carrots but loves them raw, or he might enjoy boiled rice but not risotto. Don't worry, he'll enjoy more sophisticated food as he gets older, but for now you may have better luck keeping it plain.
- **Firm crunchy textures** Lots of children react more strongly to texture than taste and often prefer foods that have a bit of bite – just-cooked vegetables, for example.
- **Separate ingredients** Some children are put off if they can't work out what's in their food – serving items so they are separate rather than mixed up can make all the difference.

The importance of healthy snacks

Small children easily flag without regular refuelling – especially once they are up on two feet and on the move. Your baby's high energy needs can be met with a small snack in between meals. You'll soon notice how quickly this revitalizes him.

It may be tempting to get out the biscuit tin, but giving him sugary snacks at this age could encourage your baby's natural preference for sweet food as well as damaging his teeth. Offering

healthy, nutritious snacks will help your baby develop good eating habits that will last a lifetime.

Rather than having food constantly available, schedule a mid-morning and afternoon snack time into your child's everyday routine. Here are some quick and easy ideas:

- a cracker with cream cheese
- chopped fresh raw fruit
- thinly sliced batons of fresh raw vegetable such as carrot and cucumber
- bread stick with hummus
- mashed banana on toasted fingers
- tiny Marmite or tuna sandwiches
- peeled satsuma segments
- chopped dried fruit such as peaches.

FUN WITH FOOD
Making food look fun can help encourage your child to try out healthy options.

Stopping breastfeeding

There's no right or wrong time to give up breastfeeding – many mothers enjoy feeding their older babies, and some successfully breastfeed and work by still giving morning and evening feeds. You may feel, however, that your baby is old enough to stop or you may simply be ready to stop yourself. You may even be pregnant again and want to wean your first child before your second arrives.

By this age, your child should be happily drinking from a cup, even if he still enjoys the comfort of breastfeeding. This should make weaning easier – although it's still important to plan ahead and take things slowly.

- Once you have decided you want to stop, stick to your decision to avoid confusing your child.
- Be consistent – start by breastfeeding only at a certain time

Caring for your child's teeth

You will need to care for your baby's teeth to prevent cavities developing. These form when the bacteria in the mouth combine with sugar in food residues left on the teeth, producing an acid which attacks the tooth enamel.

- Clean teeth twice a day with a child's soft toothbrush and a pea-sized blob of toothpaste (encourage him to spit it out after cleaning).
- Avoid sugary snacks, sweets (see page 57) and drinks in between meals and never give him sugared dummies, fruit juice or honey drinks at bedtime.
- Dilute pure fruit juices at least one part juice to three parts water and give sparingly – they contain natural sugars which can cause tooth damage.
- Offer cooled, boiled water, especially after teeth have been cleaned at night.
- Start taking your child to the dentist for a six-monthly check-up. Explain beforehand what will happen and let him sit on your lap in the dentist's chair.

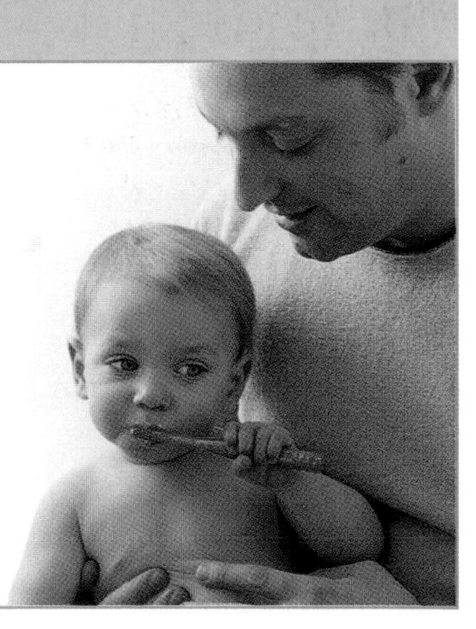

Milk needs

The amount of milk your baby is drinking at this stage will depend on him. Your older baby can drink cow's milk – although he needs a lot less milk once he is a year old: a total of 350ml (12fl oz) of whole milk per day is more than enough. If your child has too much he will feel full up and may not develop enough of an appetite for his meals.

of the day (in the evening, for example) and gradually reduce the amount of time spent on the breast.

- Avoid situations where your child expects to be fed – for example, snuggling together after lunch. Do something different instead, such as looking at a book together.
- Go together to buy a "big boy's" cup and tell him older children drink from a cup.
- When your child is tired or cranky and asks for a breastfeed to comfort him, have a distraction ready such as a new toy or quiet activity.
- Offer lots of kisses and cuddles.

Giving up the bottle

Now your baby is one year old, it's much better for his teeth and health that he says goodbye to the bottle. Milk is naturally sweet and when drunk from a bottle – especially if drunk lying down – it pools in the mouth, running the risk of causing tooth decay. Also bottle drinkers tend to eat less solid food, which may lead to eating problems later.

Some children, however, are so attached to sucking that they find it hard to accept a beaker or cup instead. You can gently get your child to give up his bottle by using some of the tips for stopping breastfeeding, as well as these ideas:

- only letting him have water in his bottle – tell him that now he's a big boy his milk has to be drunk from a beaker – this may help make the bottle less appealing
- anticipating his needs – offer drinks from a cup well before his usual time of demanding a bottle – a full tummy and quenched thirst may dampen his need for a bottle
- changing his routine – try and be out and about more in situations

Expert tip

Even though by now your child is used to firmer textures and lumpier food, he is still likely to swallow food without chewing. Don't let him run around with food in his mouth, and avoid giving him food such as whole grapes, peanuts, popcorn, whole baby tomatoes, hot dogs, uncooked peas and hard sweets.

HEALTHY FAVOURITES
Fish fingers and baked beans are full of protein and iron, and a favourite with most toddlers.

where he wouldn't normally ask for a bottle and offer diverting activities that will distract him. Changing rituals attached to bottle-feeding will help him forget about it.

Popular toddler foods

Hopefully, your toddler will enjoy eating a wide range of healthy foods, but don't worry too much if at times he isn't interested. Here are some popular toddler meals that are also healthy:

- cheese on toast offers lots of fibre and calcium
- baked potato filled with tuna is a complete balanced meal in itself
- good-quality fish fingers are packed with protein and contain some iron
- baked beans are a good source of iron and protein: choose the reduced sugar and salt variety
- grilled 100 per cent meat burgers in a soft bread roll with salad makes a healthy, iron-packed meal.

Feeding your vegetarian baby

If you and your family are vegetarian, there is no reason why your baby shouldn't be, too. It's important that he has a good supply of protein and iron: after six months, he can eat well-cooked egg yolk, beans, lentils and fish. It may also be a good idea to talk to the Vegetarian Society or your GP about iron supplements. If you are also excluding eggs and dairy produce from your baby's diet, he may need supplements of vitamins B12 and D as well as riboflavin and calcium. Consult a state-registered dietician to ensure he gets adequate nutrients for healthy development.

"We're really into food in our family – I love cooking, and Ayesha **enjoys helping.** She won't always eat what we make together, but she's more **likely to try it,** which is a step in the right direction."

RAZNA is mother to Ayesha, aged 12 months

7

Happy, healthy eating

Making sure your child has a balanced diet is easy if you follow a few simple guidelines. Helping her enjoy mealtimes and offering her fresh, wholesome food from the start will encourage her to develop healthy eating habits that will do her good not only now but into the future too.

Healthy habits

Feeding children can be a great chance to overhaul the whole family's diet. After all, your child is more likely to enjoy fresh wholesome food if she sees you enthusiastically enjoying the same food. And similarly, if you find it hard to resist a chocolate biscuit with your morning cup of coffee, your little one will be less than impressed when instead she's offered a plate of vegetable sticks to snack on! If your child is brought up to think that healthy food is the norm, it's more likely to become the habit of a lifetime.

Understanding what makes a healthy diet for your child is simpler than you may think. In fact, in many ways, the guidelines are similar for healthy adult eating - avoid too much salt, fat and sugar, limit the amount of processed food, eat lots of fresh fruit and vegetables. Monitoring what your child eats could be good for you, too!

With active, growing children, however, it's important to remember that they need more calories to keep them going and lots of protein to help them grow. So starchy food - bread, pasta, rice, couscous - has to play a major role, closely followed by meat and meat alternatives. And while low-fat, high-fibre diets may be good for grown-ups, they can be harmful for children.

What makes a balanced diet?

Making sure your child has a good healthy diet isn't complicated. You don't even need to understand a lot about vitamins and minerals. The key is to offer variety. As long as you encourage your child to eat a wide range of foods in roughly the right proportions she'll get all the nutrients she needs for healthy growth and development.

- **Carbohydrates (bread, pasta, cereals, rice, couscous)**

These are the best source of energy for active growing children and should make up 50-60 per cent of their diet by the age of five. Offer one serving at every meal.

- **Fruit and vegetables**

You can use fresh, frozen, canned or dried varieties of these.

Expert tips

- Avoid foods that are high in saturated (mostly animal) fats and have additional sugar and salt.
- Steam, bake, grill or boil foods rather than frying or roasting.
- Use as many fresh ingredients as possible.
- Give your child water or diluted fruit juice when she is thirsty.
- Offer raw vegetables (carrot, celery or cucumber sticks), fruit or bread as snacks.

What are food allergies and intolerances?

Occasionally some babies have a bad reaction to certain foods. This can be caused by either a food allergy or a food intolerance. Your baby is more likely to develop a food allergy if you or your partner suffer from allergies – but she will probably grow out of it. A food intolerance, on the other hand, means your baby will need to avoid certain foods permanently.

Food allergies

If your baby develops a food allergy, her body is reacting to a normally harmless substance and mistaking it for a dangerous one. The immune system kicks in, producing antibodies which trigger the release of histamine. This causes allergic symptoms such as a runny nose, itchy eyes, diarrhoea or a rash. In severe cases anaphylaxis occurs, a life-threatening condition that causes swelling in the mouth and throat and difficulty in breathing. Symptoms may appear within a few minutes or up to two hours after eating. Thankfully this is quite rare.

Nearly half of those children who develop a food allergy before they are three years old grow out of it by the age of seven.

Food intolerances

This is a non-allergic reaction to a food or additive. There are two common types of intolerance.

★ Lactose intolerance, which means a child can't digest the natural sugar in milk and milk products such as cheese and yogurt. Symptoms include stomach cramps, bloating, flatulence and diarrhoea. Lactose-free milk and dairy-free alternatives to milk, such as calcium-enriched soya drinks, are available.

★ Gluten intolerance (see page 28) which is caused by the protein found in certain grains such as wheat, barley, rye and perhaps oats. This can trigger coeliac disease in a small number of babies. Gluten should not be given to any baby before six months of age. Once gluten intolerance has been diagnosed, foods made with grains containing gluten - such as pasta, cereals and bread - have to be permanently avoided.

If gluten is being taken out of your child's diet on a permanent basis, it is advisable to ask your doctor for an appointment to see a state-registered dietician to ensure her diet is adequately balanced for normal growth and development.

Many supermarkets now stock a broad range of products that are gluten-free, including bread, biscuits, cereal and pasta.

TROUBLESOME FOODS
Eggs, nuts and soft-berry fruits such as strawberries are each linked to allergies in children, and bread contains gluten which can result in intolerance if given to your child too soon.

Ways to help avoid allergies

- Breastfeed for as long as possible - and, if there are allergies in the family, avoid eating potential triggers while breastfeeding. Avoiding foods which have commonly been implicated in allergies, such as cow's milk protein, eggs, nuts, wheat and shellfish may help. If you feel your diet is limited speak to your health visitor or ask for a referral to a state-registered dietician.
- Do not start weaning your baby before she is six months old.
- Delay giving your baby foods that may trigger a reaction (cow's milk, egg, wheat, shellfish, and soft-berry fruits such as strawberries) until she is at least one year old if there is a history of allergies in the family. If there are several foods being avoided it is advisable to ask your doctor for an appointment to see a state-registered dietician to help assess the diet and make sure it's providing all the nutrients your baby needs.
- Avoid nuts, especially peanuts, until your child is three years old.
- When introducing these foods - and any other new food - do so gradually and one at a time, looking out for any reactions as you go.

Aim to serve four or five portions (three meals, two snacks) a day: banana on toast for breakfast, for example, carrot batons as a snack, broccoli with lunch, and a baked peach for dessert.

- **Dairy foods (milk, cheese, yogurt)** Encourage your child to drink around half a pint of milk a day. If she's not keen, use milk in cooking and offer extra cheese, fromage frais and yogurt.
- **Meat, fish and meat alternatives** Remember to include oily fish, such as salmon, mackerel, sardines and pilchards, as well as white fish. These are essential sources of protein and iron. Lentils and beans are good meat alternatives but keep the portions small.

Extra value foods

Some foods within the four main food groups have special value.

- Breakfast cereals, if fortified, are a good source of iron and vitamins.
- Lean red meat is great for minerals, iron and zinc. Offer once or twice a week, and grill rather than fry.
- Canned sardines have lots of iron, calcium and essential omega-3 fatty acids. Serve on toast for a tasty tea.
- Broccoli is a rich source of vitamin C, betacarotene, and fibre.
- Milk can't be beaten for calcium as well as vitamin A, riboflavin and zinc.
- Cheddar cheese is a versatile source of protein, calcium and calories - use in sauces, in sandwiches, on toast or just as chunks for nibbling on.
- Bananas are energy-giving, easy to eat and packed with potassium.

Nutritional know-how

Here are some tips to help your child get the most out of her diet.

- Offer full-fat dairy products - children need a calorie-dense diet so keep low-fat yogurts and cheese, for example, for adults only. You can offer semi-skimmed milk after the age of two and skimmed milk after five.

- Avoid fibre-rich foods in large quantities - as long as your child has a portion of fruit and vegetables a day she'll be getting all the fibre she needs. Too much can cause food to move too quickly through her system, not allowing enough time for nutrients to be absorbed.
- Encourage iron absorption by offering foods with vitamin C at the same time - broccoli and baked potato with home-made lamb meatballs, for example.
- As long as your child is getting the right number of daily servings from the various food groups, she will be getting plenty of the vitamins and minerals she needs and won't need expensive supplements.

The food pyramid

The two most important food groups in your baby's daily diet are carbohydrates and fruit and vegetables. Next are protein-rich foods such as meat, pulses, and dairy products. Sugars, fats and oils should form the smallest part (the amounts that occur naturally in other foods will be more than enough).

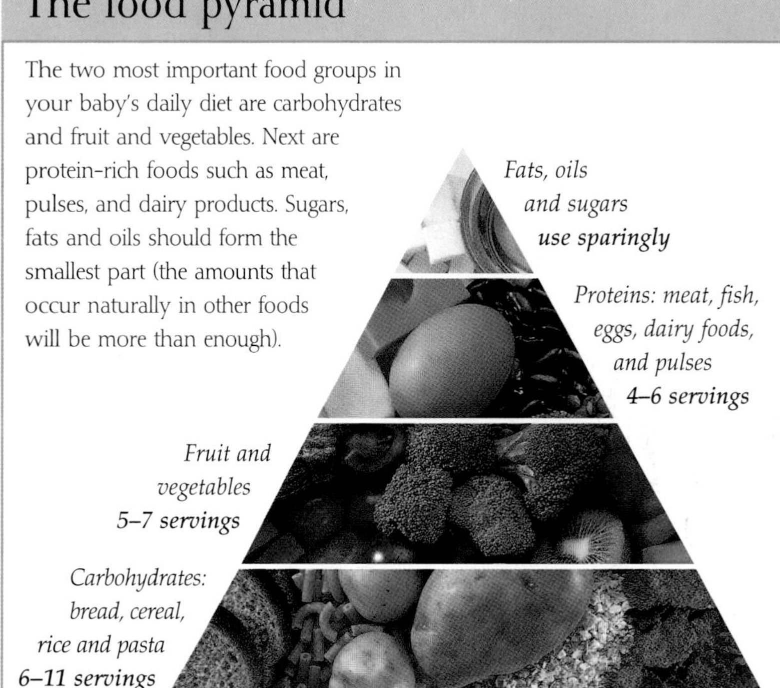

Fussy eaters

Why are some children more fussy about their food than others? There are a number of different reasons. Some children, for example, are wary about new experiences - and approach new foods cautiously. Some are unusually sensitive to certain tastes and textures. Others learn early on in their lives that they can use food to manipulate their parents and gain attention.

Understanding your child's needs will help create happy mealtimes. It's not worth trying to feed her when she is overtired, for example - little ones especially lose interest in food when they are ready for a sleep. Slow eaters need plenty of time to finish their meal and fussy eaters respond well to being offered a choice – two types of vegetables, perhaps.

Avoiding conflict

It's important to stay as calm and as neutral as possible at mealtimes. Help keep the atmosphere happy with a few simple strategies.

Sweets

Sweets not only fill your child up on empty calories - they can also damage her teeth. It would be impossible to ban them completely but you could:

- nominate a "sweetie day" – one day a week when your child can have a portion of sweets
- avoid chewy sweets if possible - opt for chocolate instead
- encourage sweets to be eaten all in one go – the impact on your child's teeth will be less if they are eaten in one hit rather than spread out over the day.

TEA PARTIES
Inviting your child's friends to tea – let her choose what to eat – can be an enjoyable occasion for everyone.

- Use some gentle persuasion – you should never force your child to eat, but if she is not eating simply because she is in a bad mood, tired or distracted then some kind encouragement can help. Most children will try a few mouthfuls because they know this isn't the same as having to eat the whole lot. Using food as a bribe ("If you don't finish your vegetables you won't have any pudding!") or a reward is not successful in the long run as it teaches a child that food can be a powerful weapon when it comes to getting what they do or don't want.

Eating out

Being prepared will help eating out be a fun occasion for all members of your family. Explain to your child what to expect and she will more than likely rise to the occasion.

- Time your outing carefully – if your child is tired or very hungry she is less likely to cope well.
- Choose a child-friendly place – lots of restaurants provide highchairs, crayons and paper, and a special children's menu.
- Take your own distractions – a favourite book or selection of small toys will help keep your child amused while she's waiting for her food or when she's finished.
- Order her favourites – your child will enjoy her meal more if she's served things she likes.

- Know when to compromise - rather than removing the whole plate of food, try to find some middle ground. If she won't eat her fish pie, for example, say, "That's fine, but you can manage your green beans, can't you?"
- Give in gracefully - there will always be times when your child just won't be persuaded to eat, in which case it's better to accept this without a fuss. Children's likes and dislikes change all the time, so tell her "I know you don't like this today - but you may next week."

Lots of children grow out of being fussy eaters. Eating with friends, for example, often encourages them to be more adventurous. And fussy children who do it for attention often give up when they don't get the response they are looking for.

The best approach to challenging behaviour or unreasonable demands is to ignore them or quietly and quickly end the meal.

Eating together

Eating together as a family is one of the best ways of encouraging your child to enjoy her food. Chatting round the table gives your child the chance to practise her social skills, and watching how you behave will help lay the foundations for good table manners. Try:

- eating together as often as possible, or at least sitting with your children while they have their lunch or tea
- getting your child involved - she can help lay the table or take a dish to the dining room - to help her enjoy the sense of occasion
- avoiding arguments - mealtimes should be a chance for everyone to relax and enjoy each other's company
- encouraging your child to join in the conversation - ask specific questions, such as "Did you play with your best friend today?"
- not to expect too much - small children don't have the patience to sit at the table for long, so once your child has finished her food let her leave the table.

Encouraging healthy mealtimes

- Provide a regular routine for sit-down meals and snacks.
- Enthuse about fresh, wholesome food – "mmm . . . this fruit salad is delicious".
- Cook one healthy meal for everyone – don't offer alternatives.
- Offer as much choice as possible – if you cook four vegetables, your child might eat two of them.
- Praise her whenever she eats up.
- Don't give up – your child may not be interested in sweet potato today, but she may well try it next week.

Weaning your baby

Helping your baby move from a milk diet to family food is simple if you follow these general guidelines. Bear in mind that if there is a family history of allergies introduction of certain foods should be delayed (see page 55).

Baby's age	Type of food	Milk and dairy products
6 months	Start with a fine semi-liquid purée mixed with breast milk, formula or cooled, boiled water, thickening it over the next few weeks.	Your baby still needs at least 600ml (20fl oz) breast milk or formula a day.
7-9 months	Mashed or chopped; finger foods, when your baby can hold things.	Your baby still needs at least 500-600ml (17-20fl oz) breast milk or formula a day; small cubes of Cheddar cheese or cottage cheese; you can now use cow's milk to mix food or add to breakfast cereals.
9-12 months	Most foods should now be mashed or chopped, and some left whole for your baby to chew on.	Your baby still needs at least 500-600ml (17-20fl oz) breast milk or formula a day; fromage frais and full-fat yogurts are fine - choose unsweetened and add fruits.
One year onwards	Your child can now eat most family food as along as it's cut up for her and doesn't contain added salt or sugar. You can now safely introduce honey to her diet.	Encourage your child to have 350ml (12fl oz) milk a day; full-fat cow's milk is now fine as a main drink.

Starchy food	Vegetables and fruit	Meat and meat alternatives
Baby rice cereal	Puréed cooked carrots, parsnips, courgette, swede, sweet potato, broccoli; puréed stewed apple or pear; mashed banana.	Once solids are established, you can start to introduce a small amount of puréed lean soft-cooked beef, lamb, pork or poultry; puréed lentils or split peas.
Try white or wholemeal bread, pasta, rice, noodles, couscous, porridge and other breakfast cereals.	Cucumber, green beans, leek, peas, mushroom, onion, sweetcorn, tomato. Citrus fruits (seedless), grapes (seedless, cut in half), mango, melon, strawberries.	Introduce a little boneless white fish (cod or haddock); hard-boiled egg yolk (no egg white until nine months); mashed, well-cooked beans and pulses.
Home-made pizza, chips, cakes, puddings and biscuits are healthier alternatives to shop-bought, which are high in fats, salt and sugar.	Encourage your baby to eat raw fruit and lightly cooked vegetables as snacks; canned fruit in natural juice is a healthy alternative to fresh fruit.	Meat and meat alternatives: sliced ham, chicken or turkey, and small chopped sausages make good finger foods; introduce boiled eggs or omelette.
Offer one serving of potato, pasta, bread, rice or couscous at every meal; limit very starchy food such as crisps, pastries or other savoury snacks.	Aim to serve four small portions a day - offer as snacks or blend into a stew or soup. Do not include nuts in your child's diet until she is at least three years old (see page 55).	Start to include oily fish such as salmon, mackerel and pilchards; trim the fat off meat and skin chicken before serving; carefully remove small bones from fish.

Useful contacts

Association of Breastfeeding Mothers
PO Box 207
Bridgewater TA6 7YT
Tel: 020 7813 1481
Web: home.clara.net/abm

British Allergy Foundation
Deepdene House
30 Bellegrove Road
Welling
Kent DA16 3PY
Helpline: 020 8303 8583
Web: www.allergyfoundation.com

British Nutrition Foundation
High Holborn House
52-54 High Holborn
London WC1V 6RQ
Tel: 020 7404 6504
Web: www.nutrition.org.uk

Child Accident Prevention Trust
18-20 Farringdon Lane
London EC1R 3HA
Tel: 020 7608 3828
Web: www.capt.org.uk

Coeliac Society
PO Box 220
High Wycombe
Buckinghamshire HP11 2HY
Helpline: 0870 444 8804
Web: www.coeliac.co.uk

Community Practitioners and Health Visitors Association
40 Bermondsey Street
London SE1 3UD
Tel: 020 7939 7000
Web: www.msfcphva.org

Institute of Optimum Nutrition
13 Blades Court
Deodar Road
Putney
London SW15 2NU
Tel: 020 8877 9993
Web: www.ion.ac.uk

La Leche League
BM 3424
London WC1N 3XX
Helpline: 0845 120 2918
Web: www.laleche.org.uk
Helpline for breastfeeding advice and information

National Asthma Campaign
Providence House
Providence Place
London N1 ONT
Helpline: 0845 701 0203
Web: www.asthma.org.uk

National Childbirth Trust
Alexandra House
Oldham Terrace
Acton
London W3 6NH
Tel: 0870 4448707
Web:
www.nctpregnancyandbabycare.com

National Eczema Society
Hill House
Highgate Hill
London N19 5NA
Helpline: 0870 241 3604
Web: www.eczema.org

Royal Society for Prevention of Accidents
Edgbaston Park
353 Bristol Road
Edgbaston
Birmingham B5 7ST
Tel: 0121 248 2000
Web: www.rospa.co.uk

Vegan Society
Donald Watson House
7 Battle Road
St Leonards-on-Sea
East Sussex TN37 7AA
Tel: 01424 427393
Web: www.vegansociety.com

Vegetarian Society
Parkdale
Dunham Road
Altrincham
Cheshire WA14 4QG
Tel: 0161 925 2000
Web: www.vegsoc.org

Index

Acknowledgments

Dorling Kindersley would like to thank Sally Smallwood and Ruth Jenkinson for the photography, Sue Bosanko for compiling the index, and Alyson Lacewing for the proofreading. Thanks also to Tanya Carr (consultant).

Models
Ilaria Pesci, Cecilia Woodhouse with Joshua, Sylvia Davidson, Kim with Carla Rabin, Keith with Anthony Blackmore, Anne with Freddie Dowland, Julia Harris and Colin with Mia Short, Tristan Smith, Jonathan Ballejo, Wendy with Jenny Cheng, Doug with Gil Krikler, Elena Marrai, Theo Angeli, Madalena Grigoletti, Avni and Alkesh with Dhanvi Shah, Dylan Ramirez, Corinna with Hannah Hyman, Lorna Zheng, Jeffrey Jaramillo, Taylor Smith, Sydney Barron, Chukwuma Orji, Phoebe Berman, Angel Kennett-Smith, Lulu with Paul and Eleanor Manitaras, Paul Bradley

Hair and make-up Louise Heywood, Victoria Barnes, Susie Kennett, Amanda Clarke

Picture researcher Anna Bedewell

Picture librarian Romaine Werblow

Picture credits Dorling Kindersley would like to thank the following for their kind permission to reproduce their photographs:
(abbreviations key: t=top, b=bottom, r=right, l=left, c=centre)
40: Science Photo Library: Mark Clarke (bl).